INDISPENSAB

INDISPENSABLE

Build and Lead a Company
Customers Can't Live Without

James M. Kerr

Humanix Books

www.humanixbooks.com

Humanix Books

INDISPENSABLE
Copyright © 2021 by Humanix Books
All rights reserved

Humanix Books, P.O. Box 20989, West Palm Beach, FL 33416, USA
www.humanixbooks.com | info@humanixbooks.com

Humanix Books is a division of Humanix Publishing, LLC. Its trademark, consisting of
the words "Humanix Books," is registered in the Patent and Trademark Office and in other
countries.

ISBN: 9-781-63006-183-8 (Hardcover)
ISBN: 9-781-63006-184-5 (E-book)

Printed in the United States of America
10   9   8   7   6   5   4   3   2   1

For Haley, Dylan, and Irene
You are indispensable to me.

Contents

Acknowledgments   ix

A Word to the Reader   xi

Prologue: Outstanding Leaders Make
Businesses Indispensable   xiii

Chapter 1: Your Business Needs to Be Indispensable   1

Chapter 2: The Right Leadership   25

Chapter 3: The Right Vision   55

Chapter 4: The Right Culture   77

Chapter 5: The Right People   103

Chapter 6: The Right Trust and Empowerment   131

Chapter 7: The Right Change Management Practices   153

Chapter 8: How to Ensure Lasting Indispensability   177

Epilogue: Just Keep It Real!   199

The Last Word   203

Notes   205

Index   213

Acknowledgments

LET ME RECOGNIZE SOME OF the people who have made a difference to me while writing this book:

> To Irene, Dylan, and Haley—thanks for giving meaning to my work;
> To my mother, Elena, and sister, Lisa—thanks for your unconditional support;
> To Burgi and the rest of the extended family—thanks for keeping me grounded;
> To my buddies, who can't be identified by name due to outstanding warrants—thanks for the study breaks along the way;
> To my editors at Humanix Books, Mary Glenn and Keith Pfeffer—thanks for believing in the value of the book; and
> Thanks to all of my clients who helped me learn and grow over the years as I continue to hone my craft.

Please enjoy *Indispensable*.

A Word to the Reader

FIRST AND FOREMOST, *INDISPENSABLE* IS a leadership book. It contains a framework, or *Indispensable Agenda*, that you can use to help you make your business one that your customers can't live without.

Indispensable is intended for one type of reader: a business professional who wants to make a difference in their organization. Whether you are a C-suite executive looking for ideas to make your business more competitive or a Gen Z new hire who is eager to establish yourself as a fresh thinker, as long as you want to make a difference, *Indispensable* is for you.

Anyone who regularly reads my Inc.com column will recognize many of the ideas and concepts gathered and presented here. Like the articles* on which it's based, *Indispensable* is written for quick consumption, fast understanding, and easy reference. Bulleted paragraphs are used to present key concepts. Ample industry examples are included throughout each chapter to help provide context and reinforce major points. I've even included a Top Ten list at the end of each chapter that summarizes its key points. I hope that you find the writing style achieves its purpose.

---

* Much of the content for this book is derived from my Inc.com column. I've combined, organized, and added additional details to some of those original posts to create an entirely new "thought piece" that is this book. That said, not all source materials from my column are specifically referenced unless used in their entirety. For more see: https://www.inc.com/author/james-kerr

Lastly, *Indispensable* is meant to be shared among colleagues and teammates. Its value comes through the building of a common understanding of what it takes to build an indispensable organization.

With that, if you're a business professional who wants to make a difference in your organization, please read on.

Prologue

Outstanding Leaders Make Businesses Indispensable

WHILE THE PANDEMIC IS STILL with us, we must find it within ourselves to focus on what we have to do to become the kinds of businesses that our customers can't live without. Yes, Amazon, Walmart, and Facebook continued to dominate their markets while other companies, like Zoom Video Communications and TeleDoc Health, leaped ahead of their competition by offering needed services in an easy-to-use framework.

Indeed, there are many great companies—only a few are indispensable.

If you're reading this book, chances are you're already the type of person who wants to lead your company to greatness. The pursuit of greatness is important, but it's not enough. Make no mistake, however—a business doesn't become indispensable by accident. Outstanding leadership is essential to bringing a company from greatness to indispensability.

This is an important distinction because anything less than outstanding leadership will not suffice. Why?

Outstanding leaders lead by example. They demonstrate desired qualities and behaviors to their followers through their actions and conduct. By doing so, these leaders put forth a sense that they and their teams share the same goals and aspirations and that together, they are going to go about achieving these ambitions as one. Indispensable businesses share a common purpose, so they need leaders who can set the example.

Salesforce CEO Marc Benioff, for example, was one of the first CEOs to lay out a plan to address the COVID-19 crisis. His eight-point plan included, among other things, a call for other CEOs to take a ninety-day "no-layoff pledge" in response to already accelerating unemployment rates—demonstrating a commitment to attending to the welfare of his people.

Further, outstanding leaders transform. They not only revitalize the organizations that they work in, but they rejuvenate the people they work with. The most preeminent leaders enable success through steady direction-setting, a single-minded sense of purpose, and unvarying communication, which facilitates the continuous transformation required to maintain indispensability.

For example, when the pandemic began to take shape, Jeff Bezos immediately pivoted attention away from his new rocket company, Blue Horizons, and placed it squarely on strengthening Amazon's online retail business. He drove the hiring of 175,000 additional workers in order to meet the gigantic flood of orders coming Amazon's way from a quarantined world—transforming the business almost overnight.

Indeed, the crisis has proven to be a great equalizer, separating outstanding companies from the rest. However, this book is not about the pandemic. Its intent is to provide you with a framework that you need to help your business become so outstanding that it befits holding the *indispensable* moniker.

As you read the book, you'll come to recognize how vital your leadership is to helping your business become indispensable. Regardless of your rank or position, you must be able to provide the following to the people you work with and serve.

A captivating vision. Outstanding leaders can articulate a vision for the future that every staff member understands and buys into. This vision becomes the stuff of rallying cries and establishes the common goal that leader and team will share.

But the vision effort must begin with understanding. If the troops don't *get* it, they won't follow. Outstanding leadership is required to articulate the vision of being indispensable and to work to drive what that means deep into the enterprise.

Active direction-setting. Next, a game plan for execution must be built in support of that vision. But building a plan without engaged direction-setting will not suffice. Outstanding leaders at every level will be fully involved, monitoring progress and charting the course for execution throughout their firm's journey to indispensability.

Enlightened coaching. Outstanding leaders support their team and understand how to provide the *right* touch at the *right* time—directive when the path to success is unclear and supportive when it's time to empower—just like any world-class coach does when building a champion.

A collaborative environment. Outstanding leaders know how to establish a collaborative tenor within their area of responsibility. Selfish and egocentric behavior is stomped out; teamwork is recognized and rewarded.

Please keep these essential behaviors in mind as you read the book. You must personify them as you enable your business to become indispensable.

Your Business Needs to Be Indispensable

MERRIAM-WEBSTER'S DICTIONARY DEFINES INDISPENSABLE AS "being absolutely necessary and not subject to being set aside or neglected." This book is written for business professionals who want their companies to become indispensable.

It provides a framework that you can follow to transform your business by first reimagining what it can be and then describing what is needed to reconstitute it in ways that make it compelling and irresistible to your customers.

This book features dozens of examples from industry, including ones drawn from Amazon, Uber, Facebook, and more. Each business example illustrates how the concepts offered in the book are already being used to make businesses indispensable in the marketplace.

Keep in mind, though, only your customers can decide if your business is indispensable. Indeed, what we think of our businesses and their ability to delight our customers is irrelevant. It is our customers who determine which businesses are indispensable. We don't get to vote on that. However, there are steps that we can take to improve our chances.

This book was written to help you build an indispensable business—one that your customers can't live without.

Why Indispensable?

The answer is simple: the competition is overwhelming.

Please believe that regardless of what your company does or how it does it, there's another firm right behind you ready to take your spot. Moreover, your competition is not just local businesses. It's global. There's no need for us to recount all the reasons why this is so. Let it suffice to remember that the internet and related technologies have made the world a whole lot smaller.

Your customers have choices. If you can't give them what they want in the ways that they want it, someone else will. It's just a point and click away. So you better figure out quickly how to become indispensable, or you just might be replaced.

Here are just a few examples of what can happen when you take your eye off the ball and neglect to strive for indispensability:

- **Boeing:** They certainly demonstrated their hubris when they worked with inspectors to certify a plane that crashed twice within months of its release. After grounding their Boeing 737 Max fleets for most of 2019, the company still has to convince the worldwide flying public that the aircraft has been appropriately modified, tested, and determined to be safe. It's unclear if the company will ever fully recover from this debacle.
- **Apple:** The stock took a tumble when it came to light that the tech giant had purposely slowed down older iPhones to force consumers to upgrade. This move forced them to offer inexpensive battery replacements to win back customers.
- **Mylan:** The drug-maker claimed it took up to a $260 million revenue hit when news came out of the possible price gauging and fixing practices related to its lifesaving allergy shot product, EpiPen.[1] Imagine the challenge that comes with having to justify a more than 400 percent price jump on a product that has an estimated 3.6 million prescriptions.[2] Mylan certainly has little care for the people relying on its products to save their life.

- **Volkswagen:** When it was discovered that the car manufacturer hoodwinked emissions testers by installing software into eleven million cars to sidestep air pollution laws, Martin Winterkorn, then CEO of Volkswagen, resigned soon after. He should have left—he lied to his customers.
- **Wells Fargo:** The fake-account scandal (highlighted by the creation of as many as two million fake bank and credit card accounts in the names of their customers) forced its stock down 10 percent when it was slapped with a $185 million fine by the government.
- **United Airlines:** Their stock plummeted after videos of a passenger being bloodied and dragged off an overbooked plane circulated on the internet and in the media. You really can't manhandle customers, even if they get argumentative.

I could go on.

The point is simple: just *do not* become one of these companies—one that misunderstands their customers or takes them for granted! There are repercussions.

Instead, learn what your customers truly want and exceed those expectations.

What Your Customers Want

Industry innovators like Apple, Amazon, and Netflix inspire other business leaders to consider ways to disrupt their respective industries. Of course, you don't have to disrupt an industry to become an indispensable business! Instead, you must be driven to excellence in all that you do and deliver what your customers want. In essence, you want to be on a constant lookout for ways to unlock your customer's potential.

Paradoxically, the key to unlocking that potential in your customers lies with the leadership and culture of your organization. These are the keys needed to differentiate you from your competitors. These are the things that will enable you to be the *provider of choice* in the hearts and minds of your customers. These will enable you to help them become disruptors of their own respective industries.

Some examples of leaders who drive winning organizations through their leadership style and focus on culture include the following:

- **Reed Hastings**, Netflix's CEO, helped create a culture based on trust that has made the company indispensable to many streaming TV viewers around the world. At the height of the pandemic, there were even memes reflecting the firm's indispensability. The world had shut down and there was nothing left to do but stay home and watch Netflix.

  The company "believes that people thrive on being trusted, on freedom, and on being able to make a difference . . . dedicated to constantly increasing employee freedom to fight the python of process."[3] By encouraging independent decision-making, Netflix allows staff to use sound judgment, not administrative policy, to delight its subscribers.

- **Jack Ma**, executive chairman of Alibaba Group (the world's largest retailer), is known for his willingness to drop whatever he is doing to assist staffers, whether, as Ma said, "it be 6 a.m. on a Wednesday, a Sunday, or during my best friend's birthday party."[4] This attitude is indicative of a leader who believes that their role is to serve their people and build a culture that leads to indispensability.

- **Satya Nadella**, Microsoft's CEO, is known for valuing his company's culture and truly empowering employees by saying, "Make it happen. You have full authority."[5] He seems to have an ever-present curiosity and is on a constant lookout for ways that others can win.

- **Virginia Rometty**, CEO of IBM since 2012, is credited with restoring the company to greatness. She believes staff development should be a primary focus, suggesting that talent development can set the stage for "changing the way work is done, using AI, putting skills at the center,"[6] which enables the company to remain vital even as digital transformation changes the business culture in which IBM operates.

- **Kent Taylor**, Texas Roadhouse CEO, gave away his salary and bonus of $800,000 to help employees during the pandemic. He also contributed $5 million to an employee emergency fund—demonstrating, through his behavior, the values that the chain espouses: "A family built on love, care, and concern. We celebrate our people in the good times and we have each other's backs in the tough times too."[7]

- **Bill Belichick**, head coach of the New England Patriots, has an unflinching commitment to a "Do your job!" philosophy that has created a winning culture at the NFL football franchise. He has led the Patriots to sixteen AFC East division titles, thirteen appearances in the AFC Championship Game, and nine Super Bowl appearances, winning a record six of them. Certainly, leadership and culture is the key to success in New England.

Why does it come down to leadership and culture?

The answer is simple: leadership drives behavior, and behavior establishes culture. Yes, that simple! Unsure on where to begin?

Just Ask Some Basic Questions of Yourself

Here are some basic questions to ask yourself about your organization. The answers to these questions will establish the platform from which you can begin to change your business and shape it into one that your customers prefer. They have been organized across several essential dimensions:[8]

On Leadership

1. What are the leadership attributes required to drive transformation to achieve your vision of becoming the provider of choice for your customers?

2. Which of the attributes do you believe are strengths among your midtier leaders?
3. Which of the attributes do you believe are weaknesses among your leadership team? How would you begin to transform these weaknesses into strengths?

On Culture

1. How is the current culture (beliefs, behaviors, assumptions) facilitating or hindering movement of your teams toward achieving transformation objectives?
2. How are definitions of responsibility, decision-making, and structure facilitating or hindering movement of your teams toward your vision?
3. How do you navigate competing internal priorities and drive innovation?

On Transformation and Change

1. Do you feel your organization is agile enough to be competitive? Can you move at the speed required to drive change with velocity? If not, what needs to be done to increase agility?
2. What is your approach to drive transformation by enhancing the customer experience?
3. What is your strategy to move your organization to optimize its interactions with its internal customers?

On Talent and Development

1. Do you think that attracting, inspiring, retaining, and deploying top talent is a priority for the firm? What are you doing to facilitate that?
2. How do you develop your team, engage and develop junior-level employees, and show you care?
3. How do you mentor staff to build high-performing and diverse teams?

On Opportunities and Innovation

1. How do you innovate at the firm?
2. How does the firm influence its industry? What more should be done?
3. How do you inspire entrepreneurial thinking and behavior?

On Breaking Paradigms that Limit Progress

1. What three things should the firm stop doing to enable you to achieve your vision?
2. What three things should the firm do to enable its leaders to accomplish transformation objectives?
3. What keeps you up at night when thinking about the state of your organization? What are you doing to address those concerns?

Clearly, it is essential to recognize that these questions are only the beginning of your journey toward creating an indispensable company that can help your customers innovate and disrupt. It is why I suggest to my clients that they adopt the Golden Rule of Indispensability and work to make it their true north.

Golden Rule of Indispensability

There are all kinds of principles that you will need to adopt to make indispensability a reality. We will present and discuss many of them throughout this book. However, there is one overarching rule that you should consider immediately, and it's this: "Do unto your customers and your staff what you'd want them to do unto you."

If you want to build an indispensable business, you must treat your customers with the utmost care. That goes for your people too. They're the ones who you're counting on to make your customers happy. This means they need to be happy too. The Golden Rule of Indispensability must be a foundation stone on which your business is *built*.

Consider how Southwest Airlines treats its employees. Besides four decades of profit-sharing, it employs a multimedia approach to acknowledging exceptional staff effort. The recognition program includes feature articles about employees in *Southwest Spirit* (the company's monthly in-flight magazine), streaming videos at worksites highlighting staffers and the work that they do, and not to mention weekly public callouts from CEO Gary Kelly praising specific employees who have demonstrated great customer service.

This kind of effort demonstrates a company's pride in its employees while embedding a strong sense of purpose in its culture. A purpose-centered culture pays dividends. Last March, just as COVID-19 was beginning to wreak havoc on the airline industry, more than twenty thousand Southwest employees signed up for unpaid time off in order to contribute to lowering costs at the carrier.[9]

It's true that the airline industry has taken quite a beating due to the pandemic. So I feel compelled to use another industry example—this one from a customer perspective—to remind us that a few decent companies have felt the impact of the virus.

Delta Air Lines works at treating its customers with respect and caring. They go the extra mile by sending personalized notes to passengers whose travel has been diverted due to weather and the like. The notes recognize the customer's frustration while offering an apology and providing a goodwill gesture in the form of additional frequent-flier points.

Perhaps the note does little to offset the inconvenience suffered by passengers. However, as the recipient of more than one of these notes, I can say it does exhibit a desire to show customers that the airline cares about their experience, even when weather gets in the way of service delivery.

A Different Mind-set Is Needed

Of course, all of this requires an openness to think differently about the customer and employee relations. The centerpiece of your new mind-set must be loyalty and fairness. You want to earn loyal customers and staff, and you want to reciprocate that loyalty by being fair and honest in all your dealings.

If you choose to create a business that operates in this way, you will become indispensable because with such values comes a whole lot of other great behaviors that will make your business the one that customers can't live without.

So make the search for *common decency* the primary goal of your policy-setting efforts by making *graciousness* and *fair-mindedness* their centerpiece. When you do, you will begin to enable the creation of a company culture that possesses high standards of propriety, good taste, and modesty. This is how leaders can weave that same mind-set throughout their enterprises.

Don't buy it? Tell me what you think when you hear these companies referenced: Hertz, Frontier Communications, Fresh Market (all in the top fifteen worst companies to work for).[10] What do you think when you hear about these companies? Southwest Airlines, Lululemon, In-N-Out Burger (all are in the top fifteen best companies to work for).[11]

I bet the ones that you like the most are the ones that have reputations for treating their people and customers exceptionally well. I bet the ones you don't like so much fail to share that same reputation for customer focus and common decency.

Yes, you must adjust your thinking to commit to live by the Golden Rule of Indispensability, but it is absolutely essential to flourish. It is the only way to turn the notion of placing "laser-like focus on the customer experience" into something more than a consultant's catchphrase. I should know—I'm a longtime consultant and use that phrase all the time! The point is, whether you know it or not, you are a service business—and, of course, your customers (and the staffers who service them) must feel like they are receiving the respect and attention that they deserve.

Every Business Is a Service Business

Indeed, every business is a service-driven business. To remain competitive, customer gratification must become the bull's-eye of your target. That said, every interaction that a customer or prospective client experiences with you matters!

The good news is that you control the situation. It's the combination of all the ways and means of how you do business that determines their experience—and it's that experience that determines whether they prefer you over any other competing product or service available in the marketplace.

Consider how easy Zappos is to do business with. The e-tailer's vast online catalog allows shoppers to search by brand, style, size, and color, among other categories. If you can't find the shoe that you're looking for at Zappos, you probably don't need it! Moreover, shipping and returns are free. They put the customer first and make each associate pledge an oath of their commitment to deliver the *wow* through service—something they call "Zappos easy."

How do you become "Zappos easy"?

Your work setting must be built to please. Have you optimized the way work gets done? Have superfluous activities been eradicated? Are you easy to do business with? Do your products and services demonstrate that you care?

They had better.

Should your customers ever get a whiff that you can't respond quickly, that you're difficult to work with, or that you don't care, they will immediately begin to look for another company to service them.

Let's take a look at some of the considerations involved should you need to revamp your work environment and improve the ways in which your customers interact with your business.

When a Renovation Is in Order

Here are some of the things that I advise when a client is considering revamping their business:

1. **Look for leverage:** Most companies have done work in the past that can be used to inform future change efforts. Look at those past efforts and determine if there is anything that can be used today. Most every change engagement that I've led has uncovered good amounts of great ideas that we can leverage.
2. **Identify quick hits:** Determine if there are any straightforward and meaningful changes that can be made quickly to demonstrate progress and represent early success for the business.

For example, this past April, as the pandemic was ramping up, Zappos revamped its customer service line to include people whom customers could call just to chat with: "Sure, we take orders and process returns, but we're also great listeners," Zappos said in a statement on its website. "Searching for flour to try that homemade bread recipe? We're happy to call around and find grocery stores stocked with what you need."[12]

It served as a reminder to staffers to always be on the lookout for ways to revamp the way work gets done, even in the midst of an international health crisis.

3. **Teach while doing:** Be sure to utilize business optimization experts on your business renovation teams. These people can impart their knowledge to project participants while the renovation work is being done, extending the capabilities of your team.

4. **Keep score:** Be sure to institute some simple metrics that can be used to map your progress as improvement ideas are being instituted.

   At Zappos, for instance, they use the "Daily Breakdown Report," which is handwritten on a central blackboard at Zappos' onsite contact center. It lists three categories of customer contacts—phone, chat, and email. Each day, someone writes the number of customer inquiries received the day before and the average time it took for Zappos to respond. It serves to inform and motivate and is a lot less formal than the call analytics systems used in traditional contact centers, which makes it feel a little less formal, yet, provides the data required to track progress.[13]

5. **Promote changes:** Encourage staffers to embrace the improvement ideas that come out of your business renovation efforts by formally communicating those ideas and recommendations to all personnel. Change efforts yield better results when their recommendations are widely broadcasted throughout an organization.

   I routinely recommend that clients follow a roll-out plan that ensures all staffers have the opportunity to discover the changes that the renovation team has unveiled and schedule for further follow-up or implementation. This promotes understanding and builds trust among staff members. No one is left to wonder what came of the change effort or what's to happen next.

6. **Provide proper attention and follow through:** Your work isn't complete when the renovation team delivers its final report. Rather, additional oversight will be needed to ensure that the recommendations are instituted.

It is no surprise that Zappos' CEO, Tony Hsieh, is a customer service zealot. He places immense value on delighting the company's customers and works to bake that mind-set into the culture. He expounds on this in his best-selling book, *Delivering Happiness: A Path to Profits, Passion, and Purpose.*[14]

Clearly, Hsieh provides the continuous leadership needed to inspire his people to deliver service above and beyond all expectations.

We will discuss more about how to manage change and optimize the customer experience in subsequent chapters. For now, let's note that laser-like focus is more than a slogan to tack up on a wall and that philosophical and process changes are needed to keep your customers coming back to you. In fact, if you do it right, you can compete quite successfully on service delivery.

How to Compete on Service

Many of my clients are surprised when I point out that there are only three ways to differentiate a business in its marketplace—*product* (think Maserati), *price* (think Walmart), and *service* (think Nordstrom). That's it!

Sure, every business needs to have strategies for all three components. However, definitive differentiation, the kind that leads to indispensability, can come from only one. Of the three, service delivery is the one that must be at least *good enough*, or your business will fail. Even Walmart, a low-cost competitor, has greeters at the door who help direct you to the "right" aisle.

So how do you begin to compete on service?

Here are the five essentials:

1. **Develop an outsider's eye:** Develop the ability to look at your business from the outside-in. What's it like to do business with you? What needs to be improved so you're the one that your customers can't live without?

    By adopting an outside-in perspective, you begin to see ways that you can become indispensable.

    Domino's is a great example of a firm that takes an outside-in POV. They've taken to help pave the streets of towns across the country to save customers' pizza from bad roads. Check out their "Paving for Pizza" campaign for more on their program.[15]

2. **Have an "in it together" philosophy:** Sadly, COVID-19 made this idea famous, though I've been touting it for years within my management consulting practice. Nonetheless, your frontline staff defines the customer experience—period. If they're good, so is your business. If not, rest assured your customers are already looking for alternatives to your products and services.

    You must encourage trust and demand cooperation among those on your front line. Trust and cooperation will not only make their jobs easier; it will begin to embolden them to keep one another honest in the delivery of impeccable service to "their" (i.e., your) customers.

    JetBlue, for example, is one of those companies that strive to be "in it together." In fact, its chairman, Joel Peterson, considers trust a key element of success. He suggests that "where there's trust, a company is free to become a whole greater than the sum of its parts. In what he calls a 'low-trust organization,' everything is harder; insecurity drives political maneuvering, individuals are less likely to put the company first, and there's a self-protective aversion to risk that limits the company's potential."[16]

3. **Hire and train compassionate people:** As mentioned earlier, you must demonstrate that you care. How do your customers experience that feeling? It's through your people, of course. Thus, it makes sense to invest in finding and developing people who can exhibit empathy and deliver the service customers expect.

There's even software that can help.

For instance, Cogito can detect emotions and speech patterns in phone conversations and then give customer service and sales agents suggestions for improving a call. A coffee-cup icon, for instance, is a signal to speak with more enthusiasm, as low-energy interactions can be seen as a sign of disrespect or a lack of interest.[17]

That's not all the software has to offer. After the insurance giant MetLife started using Cogito at its call center in Warwick, Rhode Island, for example, supervisors realized many of their agents were fast talkers when a speedometer icon repeatedly urged them to slow down.

Clearly, the tool is helping customer service agents become more engaged with customers, who are often in distress after suffering a loss.

4. **Build trust in the front line:** We'll discuss this more throughout the book. For the moment, let's agree that a properly prepared staff should be empowered to make the call on handling most mainstream customer situations. Nearly all people want to do the right thing. So train them up and let them have at it!

   JetBlue provided a wonderful example of this point when its frontline staff chose to refund a customer's fare (a bridesmaid had been dumped from the wedding party and asked for help via its social media channel).

   In fact, the carrier's customer service rep went a step further and offered, "When you're ready to patch things up, we'd like to help make your old friendship feel like new. A future girls' weekend is on us!"[18]

   Talk about a perfect response to a tough customer service situation!

5. **Push to exceed customer expectations:** Performance measurement is a thing that most companies do, but, too few do it well. Again, we explore this in more detail in subsequent chapters. Just know, if you often get subpar performance, you are likely measuring the wrong things. It's not effort that matters—it is results.

Look to establish goals and measurements of behaviors that delight the customer. Do not limit your people by inadvertently measuring them against the wrong metrics. Here are some examples of mismatched measurements:

- average handle time versus customer outcomes
- number of calls answered versus number of resolved cases
- total customer interactions versus interactions per resolution

A business that measures (and rewards) improperly (by using the wrong metrics, as illustrated above) likely has a customer service department that fields a lot of calls, short in duration, which require a ton of follow-up in order to resolve customer problems.

Alternatively, those that measure the right things are often characterized as getting customer issues addressed correctly on the first call.

At the end of the day, your customer always has other choices. Accordingly, instituting a service delivery model that truly inspires confidence from customers (especially your most discerning ones) is paramount to becoming indispensable.

That said, I can unequivocally state *indispensability is a choice*.

Indispensability Is All up to You

As a leader, you have the power within you to establish a culture that can make your business indispensable. Extraordinary integrity, high trust, focus on the customer—that's all on you. People mimic their leaders. Be the kind of leader who raises the bar in all that you do and say.

Here are some examples of the kinds of mayhem less honorable leadership behavior causes in an organization:

- **Self-centeredness:** A leader who steals the limelight, exaggerates their abilities, and needs to be the center of attention is tremendously demoralizing to staffers. Why strive when your boss steals the credit?

Consider the case of Elizabeth Holmes, founder and CEO of Theranos, for example. Her hubris led her to believe that she could do no wrong. Seeking to disrupt the health-care industry by offering cheaper and less invasive blood tests, Holmes purposely misled investors with false claims of her firm's technological capabilities. When the fraud was discovered in October 2015, she was forced to step down, and Theranos ceased to exist within three years.

Who knows what could have been achieved if Holmes was not driven to be a celebrity CEO and instead guided the firm with a slow and steady hand. Maybe her vision would have been realized.

A company is corrupted when its top leaders act selfishly. Indispensability requires a culture of cooperation and success-sharing.

- **Blame:** If a leader lacks culpability, their staff will play the blame game too.

  For example, there's no doubt that Elon Musk is a visionary leader. However, he may not be an inspiring one. His erratic interactions with critics and inexplicable behavior—calling investors names and sending outlandish tweets[19]—make many wonder if he has what it takes to make his companies indispensable.

  A leader who takes responsibility for failure demonstrates the kind of behavior that inspires others to do their best—and it's that effort that creates the best businesses on the planet.

- **Fabrication:** Should a leader operate unscrupulously on a regular basis, a culture of mistrust takes hold. This kind of culture is very difficult to reset. No one feels respected or empowered. Performance suffers as a consequence.

  Take Wells Fargo, for example. CEO John Stumpf stepped down in October 2016 following a scandal involving the bank's creation of new deposit and credit card accounts for millions of customers without their knowledge. Apparently, the behavior was encouraged by senior leaders at Wells Fargo whose bonuses were based on new accounts. While the stock remained buoyant after the scandal was reported (it's a lot of work for customers to change banks), many Wells Fargo staffers were certainly disheartened.

On the other hand, a leader who inspires trust through their actions sets the stage for an invincible culture—one capable of supporting an indispensable business.

- **Opaqueness:** If a leader fails to communicate transparently, they are promoting a culture that evades accountability and manipulates the facts.

It makes one wonder what morale must be like at Facebook, as staffers, a few years back, had to watch and listen to their CEO Mark Zuckerberg and COO Sheryl Sandberg slowly and elusively respond to public scrutiny over their slow reaction to allegations that their company was manipulated by the Russian government to influence the 2016 U.S. Presidential election.

On the other hand, staffers exude confidence when their leadership communicates in open and honest ways.

- **Unpredictability:** When a leader is unpredictable and demonstrates a willingness to bend the rules when they're not convenient to follow, they send the message that's it's OK for others to do the same.

Consider the impact on a company when its CEO or chairman is accused of sexual misconduct—which seems to continue to make headlines as the #MeToo movement continues to evolve. Recently ousted leaders like former CBS chairman Les Moonves, former McDonald's CEO Fred Easterbrook, and former Warner Bros. CEO Kevin Tsujihara appear to have been operating under a double standard. None of these men are inspiring their companies to become indispensable.

On the other hand, a leader who demonstrates great integrity and is highly consistent in their dealings brings about a culture that demands discipline and rigor in all that it does.

With all of that, should your culture lack the trust and integrity that is needed to earn indispensability in the marketplace, draw a circle around yourself. It's your behavior that dictates the actions of others around you. Recognize that it only trickles down from there.

Indeed, indispensability requires a concerted effort—both personally and throughout the enterprise. It makes continuous planning and execution central to ongoing success.

Continuous Planning and Execution

The country of New Zealand provides a great argument for continuous strategic planning and execution. In 2017, it developed a strategic plan[20] for managing a worldwide pandemic, should one emerge. The plan called for regular monitoring of world health information to identify early warning signs that a pandemic was about to commence. In 2020, as COVID-19 began to ravage the world, New Zealand was on top of it and began to execute its strategic pandemic management plan. As a result, the country was the first one on the globe to contain and eliminate the virus from its shores.

Like New Zealand, companies need to actively develop and maintain strategic plans in order to react to the subtleties of an unpredictable and swiftly changing world. A comprehensive strategic plan has the potential to propel an organization toward indispensability.

In fact, it is by making your strategic planning a regular routine—one that you monitor and adjust throughout the year—that you help your business better get ahead of—and acclimate to—the changes needed to consistently delight your customer. In fact, it can be the means by which you become indispensable.

How do you begin to make strategic planning a regular activity? Here's what I recommend to my clients.

Become a visitor. Take up the intellectual challenge of putting yourself in the shoes of a visitor to your company. You gain insight from the wider perspective that comes by seeing your business through the eyes of your customers, vendors, and other strategic partners. It gives you an edge by helping you identify better ways to execute. It enables you to better anticipate issues before they become problems.

This is what Danny Deep, the president of General Dynamics Land Systems (GDLS), the military tank–builder, does as a matter of practice. He regularly travels the world, talking with his global customers and the rest of the players who comprise the vast ecosystem that his company uses to deliver its products around the globe. His goal is to see his company through the eyes of customers and other key stakeholders. He knows that this is the only way to keep his company the combat platform solution of choice.

Push your people to see past the obvious. The same old, tired approaches only deliver the same old, tired results. Help your team think differently by regularly asking why. Why will that work? Why will customers like it? Why hasn't the competition thought of this? You're pushing them out of their *comfort zone* when you engage in this kind of dialogue with your people. You will get better strategic ideas as a result.

This is what JPMorgan Chase's (JPM's) CEO Jamie Dimon does through his "Mobile first, digital everything" mantra as he drives America's biggest bank toward becoming the clear technological leader in the banking industry.

Look to advance your operation. Ask your team what can be done to improve the way work is performed. Take those ideas and spin them into potential projects and programs that can be part of your strategic plan—refining the business and making you more competitive.

This is what Don Ishmael, vice president of manufacturing, did at GDLS. He folded the improvement ideas coming from his shop floor staff and manufacturing leaders into an Industry 4.0 program, which continues to be used as the blueprint for modernizing the way the manufacturer builds tanks.

Track results as you progress. Be sure that your performance monitoring system assesses the following questions:

- Are we putting our customers first?
- Are we better enabling our people to get the job done?
- Are we delivering improved products and services?

The answers to these questions will inform other ideas to be weaved into the strategic plan, bringing your business closer to indispensability.

Moving to make strategic planning more than an annual event offers many advantages, including enhancing your company's agility, improving its customer relationships, and bettering financial performance. Be sure to include it in your thinking as you execute your Indispensable Agenda.

The Indispensable Agenda

As you have undoubtedly come to understand, you have to get a lot of things "right" in order to gain indispensability in the marketplace. Please note, I said "right," not perfect.

In fact, chasing perfection is a fool's game. Just when you think you've got it all figured out, the game changes. Don't be fooled into thinking perfection is the only path to indispensability. It is not. However, doing things "right" is what's needed to become indispensable.

The heart of your Indispensable Agenda is instituting the following:

- the *right* leadership
- the *right* vision
- the *right* culture
- the *right* people
- the *right* empowerment and trust
- the *right* change management practices

The rest of the book delves into these essential elements of indispensability and works to demystify each one, providing you with the frameworks and practices needed to make your business indispensable.

To Close

Yes, every business aspires to become indispensable.

Here are five fundamentals that underpin many of the ideas discussed throughout the rest of the book. Keep these top-of-mind as you chart your path to indispensability.[21]

Put your customer first. This is an easy principle to embrace. If you do this, you'll likely inspire your clients to grow a fondness for your commitment to their cause—whatever that cause may be.

In the early days of Amazon, Jeff Bezos would put an empty chair in every meeting to represent the customer. It served to reinforce to everyone in that meeting exactly who they were working for and needed to exceedingly satisfy.[22]

Anticipate and solve problems before they become "big hairy" monsters. In order to do this, you absolutely have to understand your customer and be able to empathize with their situation. Prove that you can anticipate and solve problems and you will establish a level of intimacy that shows that you're someone that they can count on.

The Apple Store does a nice job with this concept. Understanding that many customers may be intimidated by the technology, Apple has instituted a customer service philosophy that incorporates the idea of listening for and resolving expressed and unexpressed needs.[23] The approach goes a long way in locking in reluctant customers to the Apple product line.

Ask for feedback. The only way to get better is to learn where there are areas for improvement and direct the effort needed to advance. Seeking feedback from your customers is one way you can better understand what is needed to become indispensable. Institute ways to solicit, understand, and use customer feedback.

Adidas' decision to make running shoes made from ocean waste was a direct result of doing something positive with its customer feedback. Besides selling more than one million pairs of shoes in the first year that the concept was introduced, the company combined two aspects of consumer demand: well-made shoes and the desire to do good for the planet.[24]

Keep your promises. This is absolutely essential to building the intimacy that you need to become indispensable. If your customer can't trust you, they don't need you. Say what you mean and mean what you say.

Geico's "Fifteen minutes or less can save you fifteen percent or more on car insurance" promise is a wonderful example of a company putting its money where its mouth is. They've done a great job of maintaining their image and keeping their promise.

Do more than you promised. Going above and beyond the call of duty is a surefire way to make your client reliant on what you bring to the party—and the greater the reliance, the more "sticky" you become. As mentioned earlier, people want to work with companies that they can trust and rely on. Doing more than what is expected is a way to exhibit your pledge to your client's success.

For example, Richard Branson's latest venture, Virgin Hotels, offers all of the amenities one would want in a higher-end hotel. However, it strives to exceed customer expectations with policies like these: no cancelation fees, no early check-in fees, and no late check-out fees. These policies exemplify a company wanting to deliver more than what has been promised.

With these fundamental philosophies in mind, let's address our first agenda item: putting the *right leadership* in place.

Chapter 1's Indispensable Top Ten List

This chapter is stacked with great content and insight. This list of the top ten takeaways is provided for easy reference. Be sure to take a deeper dive into other key concepts by reviewing the chapter in detail.

1. *Indispensable* means being absolutely necessary and not being subject to being set aside or neglected. You want your business to be indispensable to its customers.
2. Your customers have choices. If you can't give them what they want, in the way that they want it, someone else will.
3. The key to unlocking the potential of your customers lies with the leadership and culture of your organization. These elements are needed to differentiate you from your competitors.

4. The Golden Rule of Indispensability is this: "Do unto your customers and your staff what you'd want them to do unto you."

5. Every business competes across only three dimensions—product (think Maserati), price (think Walmart), and service (think Nordstrom). Certainly, strategies to cover all three elements are essential for the ongoing growth and success of any business. Of the three, service delivery is the one that has to be at least *good enough*, or your business will fail.

6. Be sure to establish goals and measurements that deliver customer delight, and don't limit your people by inadvertently measuring them on the wrong things.

7. A leader who takes responsibility for failure demonstrates the kind of behavior needed to create a culture of integrity.

8. A leader who prepares their team and empowers them to make good decisions (and helps them learn from their mistakes) establishes a culture of trust—one where the individual feels safe to do their best.

9. Keep your promises to build the customer intimacy that you need to become indispensable. If they can't trust you, they don't need you.

10. The path to indispensability, includes the *right* leadership, the *right* vision, the *right* culture, the *right* people, the *right* empowerment and trust, and the *right* change management practices. Each must be fine-tuned for your company to become indispensable.

CHAPTER 2

The Right Leadership

OUR FIRST AGENDA ITEM IS about doing what you have to do to put the right leadership in place.

One is not a leader simply due to title, pedigree, or a conspicuous place on an organization chart. I believe, instead, that leaders are built on a foundation rich in character, which enables them to inspire others to follow. Exceptional leaders not only possess the requisite honesty and righteousness needed to gain followership, but they emanate the hunger and conviction needed to motivate others to do great things.

I'm not alone in this belief. In fact, Norman Schwarzkopf once said, "Leadership is a potent combination of strategy and character. But if you must be without one, be without the strategy."[1]

As outlined at the end of the last chapter, leadership is one of those things that you have to get *right* in order to become an indispensable organization. In fact, I suggest that indispensability starts with exceptional leadership, and exceptional leadership begins with character.

Leadership Begins with Character

Drawing a connection between leadership and character is not all that profound. Don't we all want our leaders to be of honorable character? The idea seems universal to me. Here's why:

- **We believe those whom we trust:** You're not going to follow someone who you don't trust. Sure, you'll likely do your job and work on an assignment from a boss you don't trust. However, that boss won't get your best effort, especially when things get tough.

  Building an indispensable *business* is tough work. Leaders who lack character won't get you there because the people they lead may not consistently deliver their best effort.

- **Consistency inspires confidence:** We gain confidence in leaders who are consistently fair, honest, and reliable. While we may not always *love* every decision made by such leaders, we continue to respect and admire those who are consistent. Indispensability requires consistency among your leaders.

  Marc Benioff, founder, chairman, and co-CEO of Salesforce, is known for his leadership consistency. More specifically, Benioff has been consistent in following through on his company's commitment to its social impact and responsibility values. Closing the gender wage gap and boycotting Indiana after the state's controversial "religious freedom" law are just two recent examples of a leader taking a stance on societal issues.[2] Such examples inspire confidence among staff that Benioff is committed to the firm's core principles, and through his actions, he is subtly inspiring employees to be committed too.

- **Conviction draws attention:** A leader with conviction generates a kind of allure that is difficult to ignore. Think of Jobs, Musk, and Bezos, and you'll get my point. Leaders of high character believe in what they're saying and project the conviction needed to rouse their people into action.

- **Passion turns us on:** It's mightily attractive to be in the moment with someone who is passionate about what they're doing. It inspires your best effort. Leaders who are passionate about making their organizations indispensable tend to create those kinds of moments.

  Steve Jobs is noted for the passion that he brought to his work at Apple. He said that the secret of business success is to have a passion for what you do. His belief centered on the notion that attaining success is so hard that if you don't love what you do and have the ability to sustain that passion over a long period of time, you'll just give up.[3]

Clearly, Apple is one of those companies that many would argue is indispensable. Just ask your teenage daughter if she can live without her iPhone and you'll understand what I mean!

- **Indispensability demands courage:** People want their leaders to stir them to take action. But this is no easy task. It requires tremendous courage to stir up the enthusiasm needed to drive an idea as big and expansive as indispensability. It takes even more courage to make all the hard decisions needed to realize that vision. Leaders must possess the personal character and courage to motivate while staying the course.

  Like every other restaurateur in the United States, Wolfgang Puck was not immune to the ravages that the pandemic had on his businesses (Wolfgang Puck Fine Dining Group, Wolfgang Puck Catering, and Wolfgang Puck Worldwide, Inc.). It took courage for him to pivot away from his core restaurant and food preparation businesses and seek new revenue streams.

  In a recent interview with Boris Groysberg, a professor of business administration at Harvard Business School, Puck offered, "I'm giving home shopping a try and it's going well. We've sold over 11,000 of our air fryers and $360,000 worth of steaks . . . I have my catering chefs and everybody working with me. That's what made it possible to recently do $2.5 million worth of business on a weekend."[4]

In a nutshell, extraordinary leaders possess a certain *je ne sais quoi* that makes them distinctive and impossible to ignore. To gain indispensability, we need leaders who hold the necessary allure to inspire others to follow. But remember, leadership is not management. Often confused for one another, these are two very different things.

Leadership Is Not Management

Clearly, leadership and management are strongly related—and managers can certainly lead, and leaders can certainly manage—however, the skills required to be exceptional at either one are explicit and pure. We need great leaders to drive a company to indispensability.

Here are a few key distinctions worth noting:[*]

1. **Mangers prefer the black and white; a leader can live in the gray.**

   By definition, abstract thinking enables a person to make connections among, and see patterns within, seemingly unrelated information. The ability to think abstractly comes in very handy when reimagining how an organization can become indispensable. Conversely, a manager must be able to work with, and analyze, concrete data in order to ensure optimal results as the organization evolves through its journey to becoming something their customers cannot live without.

   Steve Jobs serves as a wonderful example of a leader who has patched together different ideas to create something wholly new out of them. Remember, he led the team that was able to rethink the telephone—turning it into the all-purpose communication and entertainment device that it is today.

2. **A leader reimagines what can be; a manager administers change.**

   A leader must set direction and inspire people to follow them. They do this by reimagining the possibilities. It's the manager's job to direct the work needed to realize the intentions set forth by the leader.

   Elon Musk is one of those kinds of visionary leaders who inspires people to follow. Look what he did at SpaceX. It is an important touchstone for redefining the dream of space travel. It is a testament to the power of a leader's world-changing business vision.

3. **A leader determines the destination; a manager drives their team to reach it.**

---

[*]   The following list is derived from my article "Leader or Manager? These 10 Important Distinctions Can Help You Out," Inc.com, August 10, 2015.

A leader defines the target. An exceptional manager does whatever it takes to hit it.

Richard Branson is one of those kinds of leaders. He doesn't get into the weeds, preferring instead to define the goal and let his team determine how to get there. He deliberately practices discussing future ideas with his team because, he believes, it inspires his Virgin employees to figure out the best way to achieve his vision. He calls it "talking ahead of yourself."[5]

4. **Management requires blind commitment to completing the task at hand; leadership requires confidence in the face of uncertainty.**

A leader's life is filled with uncertainty. They're setting a course to indispensability for their company in unchartered waters. Once the course is set, managers are duty-bound to follow the stated direction and commit to delivering the results expected.

Consider Jeff Bezos's tenacity and confidence when starting Amazon. The company finally turned a profit in 2003, which was nine years after being founded and seven years after going public. Like him or not, Bezos serves as a great example of a leader who can maintain confidence in the face of great uncertainty.

5. **Leaders articulate; managers translate.**

A worthy leader can describe their vision in vibrant detail so as to engage and inspire their organization to pursue it. A solid manager must interpret that vision and recast it in terms that their teams can understand and embrace.

Bob Iger, Disney's CEO, made his commitment to his vision for Disney+ clear in an email that he sent to all two hundred thousand Disney employees after his February 2019 earnings report: Disney's direct-to-consumer business, he wrote, "remains our number one priority." From all indications, the service's successful launch in November of that year continues to give Netflix a run for its money.

6. **Managers look for specifics; leaders imagine the possibilities.**

A prodigious leader can inform their ideas by providing a compelling vision for becoming indispensable. It helps them help others "see" what can be. Managers must understand that vision and translate it into the specifics needed to execute.

Troy Clarke, the recently retired president and CEO of Navistar International, developed a vision for his company, the makers of International Trucks, just before handing over the reins to his successor, Persio Lisboa (Navistar's former COO and twenty-year veteran of the company).

Called Vision 2025, the vision places emphasis on the customer and calls for greater investments in technology as a means of gaining back market share lost in recent years due to customer's concerns over product reliability. Lisboa has committed that he and his management team will use the vision to guide their decision-making[6]—already announcing Navistar will begin selling driverless semis in 2024, for example.[7]

Clarke is an example of a leader imagining the possibilities and leaving a legacy as a result.

7. **Leaders sell; manages instruct.**

A leader must sell their vision for indispensability to their organization and its stakeholders. They must convince all concerned parties that what is envisioned is achievable and provides greater value than any other conceivable alternative. In keeping, a manager must be able to teach their teams what must be learned and adapted to attain the objectives described in the vision.

Consider Mark Zuckerberg's achievement with Facebook. His idea was hatched in his Harvard dorm room in 2004. Today, Facebook is worth nearly half a trillion dollars and is clearly the most popular social network on the planet. It took a lot of selling to create an organization that could achieve this much in so little time.

8. **Managers understand how work gets done; leaders look to the outside world for inspiration.**

A leader must understand the business environment in which the enterprise operates so as to better anticipate opportunities and avoid disaster, while a manager makes sure that work gets done inside the business.

Reed Hastings, cofounder, chairman, and CEO of Netflix, is a leader who took his understanding of future trends to build a business that many people can't live without today. He saw that people would much prefer to download or stream their entertainment from home rather than go to a brick-and-mortar store and deal with renting and returning hard media. Under his leadership, Netflix is a powerhouse.

9. **Leadership requires risk-taking; management requires restraint.**

A leader will take educated risks when setting a strategic direction for a business. Managers must have the self-discipline to stick to the plan for realizing that strategic direction so as to ensure that the strategy comes together as planned.

Sara Blakely, founder of Spanx, is a leader willing to take some risks. She bootstrapped her business from personal savings and built a multiline company that has become synonymous with revolutionary body-shaping undergarments.

This is an example of what it takes to create an indispensable business.

10. **Leadership is accountable to the entire organization; management is accountable to the team.**

Finally, leaders must consider the impact of their decisions on the whole organization. A misstep can bring an entire business to its knees. It's an enormous responsibility. Correspondingly, managers are responsible for their teams. They must ensure that their teams are prepared to deliver and that each member is equipped to do what is required for success.

Clearly, the leaders discussed in this section are accountable for the ongoing success of their respective businesses. Even if their managers fail to execute, it is the likes of Hastings, Bezos, and Iger that must be responsible for ensuring that their companies continue to flourish. Indispensability requires this kind of accountability.

That said, there are important differences between leading and managing. The best leaders lead and let others manage; the best managers understand their leader's vision and work with their teams to achieve it. Your indispensable business needs both. Take the time to understand the differences that exist between the two and accept no cop-outs, or rationalizations, from your entire leadership team for not doing what is needed to succeed.

Common Leadership Rationalizations

A leadership team determines the *personalty* of their companies. Find a firm that is unwavering in their pursuit of indispensability and you'll find leaders who are steady and resolute in their determination to be outstanding in all that they do. Similarly, find a company that is unpredictable and inconsistent in its execution and you will find leaders who are fine with subpar performances.

What causes the difference? It's a phenomenon that I see quite often in my work as a leadership coach and management consultant. When hired to help fix a leadership problem, inevitably we find that leaders choose to justify their lackadaisical leadership practices in a variety of ways. In my opinion, every excuse is simply a rationalization.

These are the most common:

1. **I've paid my dues.** This indicates that the leader feels that they are among the privileged, so they're above having to do any work. You want leaders who put the customer first and have the poise and confidence to be effective in all circumstances. Taken to the extreme, disaster can result.

   Kmart went bankrupt, for example, because of this kind of leadership cop-out. Their then chairman Charles Conaway and president Mark Schwartz thought that they were deserving of more. They misled shareholders and company officials about the company's looming financial troubles, choosing instead to allegedly squander millions of dollars of the company's money on luxury items for themselves. When Kmart filed for Chapter 11 in 2002, it was the third largest such filing at that time.

2. **Who has time for this "motherhood and apple pie" stuff?** This points to a leader who thinks that employee engagement is unimportant and a waste of time. You want leaders who understand the need for, and are comfortable articulating, a vivid and compelling vision story—one that gives people something to aspire to.

3. **Their paychecks should be motivation enough.** Related to the earlier rationalization, this one reveals a leader who lacks the emotional intelligence to recognize the need to motivate and inspire. You want leaders who can instill confidence in their team—the kind of leader whom people want to work with.

    PepsiCo CEO Ramon Laguarta does things the other way. He takes care of his people to motivate them. During the height of the coronavirus outbreak in early 2020, he ensured that employees who produce, transport, or deliver its products received at least an extra $100 per week. He also adopted a policy of providing full salary for fourteen days for any employee who was quarantined and provided at least two-thirds of regular pay for up to ten weeks for those who were sick with the virus or caring for a loved one with the virus.[8] It's that kind of caring that promotes followership.

4. **I expect them to do whatever they have to do to get it done.** This expresses a leader's willingness to bend the rules in the name of achieving goals. You want leaders of high integrity who model the kinds of behaviors that you expect from your team.

    Mark Zuckerberg's handling of Facebook's role in the Russian interference and Cambridge Analytica scandals illustrate this kind of leadership cop-out. While he took responsibility for what he called a "breach of trust," he was still willing to pass the buck as to how Facebook ever got into these situations in the first place, suggesting that he not testify at congressional hearings on the matter because, as he put it, "there are people at the company whose full-time jobs are to deal with legal compliance or some of these different things, and they're just fundamentally more in the details on those things."[9]

While that's undoubtedly true, his implication that he didn't know anything about the fact that his company sold ads to Russia's Internet Research Agency and unwittingly became a Russian propaganda machine as a result is a bit too much to accept. It's not some legal compliance staffer's job to monitor growth and understand where it comes from, it's the CEO's job.

5. **I like to get in the weeds.** This shows a leader who lacks trust in their team's ability to do it "right." You want leaders who are sincerely interested in the work and inspire their teams to do their best. You don't want ones who lack confidence and feel compelled to micromanage.

6. **I don't need to be involved.** The polar opposite of the previous rationalization, this leader has checked out and does not provide leadership. You want leaders who can teach their people how to be the best that they can be.

   In fact, research shows that while the impact of absentee leadership takes longer to develop, it can damage employee job satisfaction for a couple of years after a change in leadership. Simply put, absentee leadership creates the kind of job stress that requires a long time for recovery.[10]

7. **I have an open-door policy.** While this sounds nice in practice, this is a classic rationalization because the burden is on the employee to seek out guidance. You want proactive leaders who are always involved and pushing their people to be better.

8. **They don't need to know the plan.** This illustrates a leader's desire to withhold information from their team. You want leaders who promote transparency and can communicate effectively so that there is no doubt about what is important.

   Google cofounders Larry Page and Sergey Brin used to host weekly all-hands meetings that covered prior-week updates, product demonstrations, new hire callouts, and thirty minutes of Q&A. It was a great way to ensure that staffers knew what was going on in the company.

But the firm is doing away with this under its new leader, Sundar Pichai, who reportedly sent an email to employees attributing the reason for eliminating the weekly call to, among other things, meeting leaks.

It's unclear what effect this type of move will have on already present workplace tensions, but I can't imagine that it will help improve Google's famously open work culture.

9. **Their job is to make me look good.** This exemplifies a narcissistic leader, one who believes that their success is more important than that of their business. You want leaders who are involved and connected to the people they lead. You want ones who service their team and make them successful.

10. **If they want compliments, they're in the wrong business.** This points toward a leader who feels that providing positive feedback makes them look weak. You want leaders who recognize accomplishments and reward people for exceptional performances.

Tom Mendoza, the recently retired vice chairman of NetApp (a cloud services and data management company headquartered in Sunnyvale, California), did it right. He would call ten to twenty employees every day to thank them for "doing something right." He asked his managers to notify him of the names of people doing good work from their areas in the company, and then he would make his calls. It's no wonder the firm has ranked in the Fortune 500 since 2012.

Before we move on, please promise yourself to take a moment and readjust your thinking if you ever find yourself using any of these common rationalizations. After all, it is that very moment that your people likely need your leadership the most. Instead, think of ways to build a team of leaders. You'll need a team of leaders to drive indispensability into your organization.

How to Build a Team of Leaders

Building a team of passionate leaders begins with proper preparation. Once your people are properly prepared, they can be put into positions that enable them to make decisions that count. This positions you to enhance trust throughout the enterprise and build authentic commitment to the cause of becoming indispensable in the marketplace.

Of course, you need to be mindful of investing the time and energy required to develop your team of leaders. They must be at the highest levels of competency so that you can entrust them with making the "right" calls nine times out of ten. Once they're ready, you can let them do their thing.

Here are some ideas to drive your team of leaders to greater heights of proficiency:

1. **Teach as you lead.**

Don't be afraid to show your team what good looks like. Regularly take the time to gather your team together and share with them some insights about what underpins a few of your recent decisions. You can build higher competence within your team when you teach as you lead.

Koji Yoshida, the former CEO of Mitsui Sumitomo Insurance Group's U.S. division, was a master of this kind of interactive leadership. His weekly management huddles, held during the height of the merger of the Mitsui and Sumitomo insurance operations, featured him assisting his newly merged leadership team to better understand the key decisions that he made in the past week. He placed particular emphasis on examining the different things that went into his decision-making process as a way to teach while leading. Completed in just about twenty minutes per week, the approach helps in developing the next generation of leaders within his team while improving transparency and trust among the group.

You can use this kind of approach when empowering your team to do what it takes to improve indispensability. You can emphasize the importance of considering alternatives, evaluating risks, and thinking through important implications. Undoubtedly, this kind of teaching-while-leading process will help your team make better decisions.

2. **Join forces on "decision rights."**

It can be challenging to build a team of leaders. Sometimes people are uncertain about what they're responsible for and question if they have the right to make certain business decisions. That said, it's essential that you, together with your team, reach a mutually agreed-upon set of conditions for when team members can act independently and which situations require your involvement or approval.

I recall working on a recent reorganization effort at GDLS, when the company's then president Gary Whited and its CHRO Heather Wade identified this very issue as their single greatest source of consternation in the change effort. They knew that we had to get this right in order for the company to continue to execute and deliver on its customer obligations.

Ultimately, we ran several workshops with each of the three key market leaders and their newly minted teams to ensure that everyone understood exactly who had the authority and responsibility to make decisions in the new organizational structure.

Joining forces on decision rights and escalation parameters provides your team with the "bowling alley gutter bumpers" that they need to learn the ins and outs of leading while limiting risks to the business as it actively pursues its agenda of indispensability.

3. **Eradicate *pocket vetoes.***

If the U.S. Congress gives the president a bill and the president doesn't sign it, the bill isn't passed. He didn't reject the bill, per se, he just didn't take any action, so it died on the vine. That's a pocket veto. Don't do that to your team when they make decisions.

Instead, use any subpar decision-making as a learning opportunity for your team. Talk to your team about how to make a better decision the next time a similar situation arises. It will improve their performance, and you will build a stronger and more resilient team as a result.

These kinds of ideas can become the backbone of developing your leadership talent, especially the newly minted managers who will undoubtedly play major roles in transitioning your firm to indispensability in the marketplace.

Tips for the Newly Minted Leader

Business has gotten faster, and your need to make quick decisions seems to have grown exponentially in the era of the World Wide Web and smartphones. But don't let this seeming "need for speed" rush you into making poor decisions. Here are a few leadership tips, especially nuanced, for managing the blitzkrieg of demands that can come your way as a newly minted senior leader:

1. **Time is your friend:** It's funny how often we stress out over things that seem so insurmountable at the time, only to find that with time, our stress is unfounded. Indeed, time can be your friend as a new senior leader. Issues often work themselves out without much intervention if you just give the situation the time needed for the dynamics to change. You want to be sure to give you and your team the time needed to collaborate, to think, and to decide on the best course of action.

   When the pandemic began to take its toll on businesses around the globe, Quinn Snacks CEO Kristy Lewis didn't over-react to the situation. Rather, the leader of this growing farm-to-bag food business took her time and decided to stay the course, stating in an interview at the time, "We are leaning in to just being us. Just real people on a mission to do good in the world, and we are going to tell that story in a way where it connects us to *all*. How do we connect to the families and people buying Quinn? . . . Show up during their life and support them as best we can."[11]

   That's good advice for any indispensable business, regardless of the circumstances. New leaders need to learn how to slow down and take the time to get it right.

2. **Less is more:** This oxymoron is worthy of your consideration. Information is a valuable commodity. Give too much, and it can be

used against you. Yes, transparency is a fundamental that should never be skirted. However, be careful and thoughtful in your messaging—work to be clear and concise when giving direction and addressing issues. But don't be in a hurry to explain every gradation or implication of what you just said. Your community of stakeholders will ask questions if they don't understand your intent. But stay on point—many a leader has brought their team to a screeching halt by overexplaining every thought that's ever entered their mind when making a decision.

3. **You don't have to answer just because "they" called:** Bombarded with questions and issues from every direction, every day, many leaders become extremely reactionary—feeling compelled to immediately answer every question or email that comes their way. Stop!

   This is an issue for many of the younger executives whom I coach. They seem compelled to answer every email. My counsel to them is to *slow down*, going so far as to offer them ideas for physical cues that they can use to self-regulate. One woman I work with now keeps an elastic band around her wrist that she can snap whenever she feels stressed by the piling up of unanswered calls and emails. It reminds her that it's OK to let some things wait before responding.

   In fact, if you surround yourself with a great team that can help you address what needs to be done, then learn to delegate and use your team to respond to some of the calls and messages that you receive.

4. **Silence is a tool:** In fact, it has been said that it is golden! Sometimes a request doesn't deserve a response. In fact, by not responding to some requests, you are sending a message. Just be sure that your use of silence is used deliberately, and you'll develop another vital messaging tool.

   Consider JFK's efforts during the Cuban Missile Crisis. Besides being under immense pressure and challenging time constraints, Kennedy didn't escalate the situation into another world war through hasty decision-making and incessant negotiation. Instead, he maintained composure and went silent for forty-eight hours when Prime Minister Khrushchev sent a letter to him stating a willingness to remove the missiles from Cuba in exchange for a U.S. promise not to invade the island. Kennedy used that time to pull his team together to determine a path forward that allowed both countries to avert a nuclear war.

5. **Sometimes you need to go slow in order to go fast:** I've saved the best for last. This bit of advice is priceless when feeling the pressure to move out. If you go too fast, too quickly, you and your team may fail to put the necessary infrastructures in place that are needed for long-term success.

Interestingly, a *Harvard Business Review* article reported on some provocative research that backs up this point. In the piece, the authors wrote, "In our study of 343 businesses (conducted with the Economist Intelligence Unit), the companies that embraced initiatives and chose to go, go, go to try to gain an edge ended up with lower sales and operating profits than those that paused at key moments to make sure they were on the right track. What's more, the firms that 'slowed down to speed up' improved their top and bottom lines, averaging 40% higher sales and 52% higher operating profits over a three-year period."[12]

So don't be in a crazy rush to immediately "fix" every issue that springs up. Instead, work on going slow to go fast. You'll need this capability in your repertoire on your journey to indispensability. Of course, developing the *right* amount of audacity can also help you drive needed change too.

On Becoming a More Audacious Leader

A certain amount of audacity is needed if you're going to lead your company to indispensability. That said, if you tend to be conservative in your decision-making, I suggest that you become aware of the importance of working on becoming more fearless.

Fearlessness is a critical trait to develop for several reasons, including the following:

1. **Success gets throttled when leaders fail to lead.** Making decisions is a vital element of leading. If you aren't making decisions in a reasonable time frame, your team will find it difficult to proceed in its pursuit of becoming indispensable. Your lack of decisiveness will raise insecurities in your staff.

   Consider the audacity that NBA commissioner Adam Silver demonstrated when he announced in March of last year, well in advance of any governmental shutdowns, that he was suspending play for the remainder of his league's season. In hindsight, Silver's decision has proven to be quite courageous and wise, given all of the chaos that transpired in other professional sports since that time.

   So work on trusting your gut. After all, you've been put into this position because of your experience and ability to lead. Your gut instinct is usually something that you can trust.

2. **Your reaction time slows proportionately with your fear of failure.** If you typically have a fear of failure, it's likely that your decision-making is very slow and meticulous. Your firm's responsiveness suffers as a result, and that can have a negative effect on your brand. It's hard for a business to be considered indispensable if it has a reputation for sluggishness.

   A way to overcome your fear of making the wrong decision is to adopt a new philosophy—one that makes it acceptable to make mistakes as long as lessons are learned and those same mistakes are never repeated. This enables you to establish a "learning organization," too. This will improve your reaction time and improve morale among your staff as well. Your team will gain confidence as you encourage them to make well-informed decisions within their spheres of responsibility.

3. **A lack of decisiveness leads to missed opportunities.** It's highly likely that you are missing many opportunities to grow and mature your business whenever your decision-making stalls.

   Did you know that Yahoo almost took over Facebook back in 2006? Yahoo's CEO Terry Semel had a handshake with Facebook's

Zuckerberg for a $1 billion buyout before Semel tried to back out of the deal, making a counteroffer of $800 million. Several weeks later, when the original $1 billion was back on the table, Zuckerberg put a kibosh on the deal. What an example of a missed opportunity!

Remember, there's a good chance that your competitors are moving forward while you're mulling over your next move. So work on making the call and take advantage of the opportunities to become more indispensable in the marketplace.

4. **Breakthrough thinking stalls.** If you're someone who tends to fall victim to *analysis paralysis*, you are probably stifling the breakthrough thinking capabilities of everyone within your span of control too.

   It's better for you, and your business, to begin to adopt a different approach to decision-making—one that places an emphasis on gathering necessary facts as quickly as possible and swiftly moves towards action. Exhaustively dedicating time to evaluate every conceivable scenario wastes time and fatigues the organization.

5. **The fear of the unknown suffocates innovation.** Innovation is the art and science of creating something that wasn't there before. You may be crushing all innovative thinking within your business if you fear the unknown.

   Strive to make your best decision based on the information available, then monitor and adjust as you move on. Don't stifle new ways of thinking and doing—those could be the very things needed to become indispensable.

   Encouraging dissent is another attribute of an audacious leader. In fact, it is a characteristic that most great leaders share.

Encourage Dissent*

If there was only one operating principle that I could impart to you and your team that should magically be embraced and flawlessly practiced from now on, it would be this:

Everyone on the team has an obligation to express their dissent.

---

* This section is based on my article: "Want to Improve Teamwork at Your Company? Encourage Your Employees to Disagree With You," Inc.com, November 27, 2018.

The implications for your team in implementing this leadership principle are obvious. Indeed, not only do your people have *permission* to speak up when they don't agree with a new concept or idea—they have a *duty* to express that opposition. In fact, if your people have dissenting opinions and they fail to share them, then they are not fulfilling their responsibilities and run the risk of losing their spot on the team.

The implication for you, as the leader, is less clear. But it is just as important. Truly, if you don't encourage the expression of disagreement and you fail to listen to your team when they do, you will soon be leading a team of people who do not think. Why should they?

Clearly, this is not the kind of leadership needed to become indispensable. Here are a few ways that you can establish a work setting that encourages the expression of dissenting opinions:

1. **Make it about the idea, not the person.**

   The expression of opposing ideas can quickly escalate out of control when people's egos get in the way of active listening. Indeed, one's need to be "right" can supersede the desire to get to the "right" answer. So if you see a discussion involving differing points of view beginning to get personal, it's time to step in and remind all involved that the conversation is about ideas, not about discrediting the people who express them.

   A colleague of mine has gone so far as to institute an active listening protocol: the teams that she works with are required to repeat the idea that was originally posed before offering a dissenting opinion. This keeps the focus on the idea and not on the person. Her meetings tend to be appreciated for their energy and positive vibe.

2. **Let them know that you're not above being challenged.**

   Let it be known that you've got your "big boy" or "big girl" pants on and that you can handle the fact that your team may have an opposing idea—and that there will be no repercussions, implied or direct, should a team member express their disagreement with your idea. Reiterate to them that you're not looking for sycophantic agreement; you're looking to discover the best idea.

A former mentor of mine was brilliant in demonstrating this behavior. He would thank team members whenever they challenged his thinking, often saying, "Thank you for pushing back. This is how we all get better." His leadership style continues to influence me to this day.

3. **Adjust the job requirements.**

Make it clear to your team that it is a job responsibility for them to bring their best ideas to work every day, and expressing differing points of view is part of the job requirement. You can really hammer home the point by suggesting that failure to do so puts their future on the team in peril.

Of course, dissent for the sake of being uncooperative is not the intent. Rather, you want to ensure that differing ideas are expressed in constructive ways and that the primary driver is a thirst for deriving the best answer.

I have a client who has done an exceptional job of reestablishing job requirements by adding the line "Must be comfortable expressing opposing points of view in a collaborative setting" to all of her team's job postings. She believes that it puts this less-than-obvious job expectation front and center. I tend to agree.

4. **Change the discourse.**

Most work-related meetings are pleasant and polite. As a consequence, many lack substance or lead to results. It's one of the reasons that so many people complain about the time wasted each week in meetings.

Let's change the conversation. It's time to make it clear that sharing differing points of view is how the game of business is won. One of my clients has taken on the role of provocateur with his top leadership team meetings. He purposely takes an extreme position on certain topics as a means of invoking a response from his people. It's clear to me, as an honorary member of his executive team, that once the ice is broken, and someone challenges him, open and honest communication ensues.

5. **Make it a teaching moment.**

Truth be known, it is likely that some opposing ideas will lack merit right out of the gate. Use those occasions as a teaching moment. Seize the opportunity to teach them why some ideas may not work in practice. They'll get stronger as they learn, and you'll build additional trust by demonstrating that you hear them and are willing to offer additional insight to improve their thinking.

My executive coaching clients provide me with the opportunity to do this on a regular basis. It helps me help them fine-tune "true north" for their businesses while demonstrating the kinds of leadership behaviors that they should adopt to establish a true *learning organization*—one that is seen as indispensable by their customers.

Indeed, encouraging dissent is a characteristic of a strong and capable leader. It's a great way to keep things simple—your team learns that the goal is to help the business succeed. The goal is not to be right all the time. If you want to "keep it real" at work, keep it simple.

Keep It Simple

Let me share a word of caution for those of you trying to establish your own personal leadership style. Keep it simple. It is very easy to become overcome by all of the grandiose ideas that so many leadership pundits offer up in their latest books. I like to focus on the familiar and practical. It's gotten me this far, and I don't suspect that I'm going to change my approach to offering practical advice, regardless of the latest management fad.

In my last leadership book, *It's Good to Be King*,[13] I offer more than sixty straightforward and easy-to-apply leadership tips. At the risk of being accused of shameless self-promotion, let me offer up my top ten tips for keeping leadership simple. My aim is to share something that every leader can quickly use as they go about the work of making their firms indispensable.

Here is my top ten list of tips for keeping leadership simple:

1. **Leading is a choice—don't squander it.** When it comes time to lead, you can rise to the occasion or let someone else take charge. Either way, you live with the consequences of that decision. If you choose to rise to the occasion, do it deliberately and with foresight of action. Don't just wing it.

2. **It's almost never too late to right the ship.** Even when the situation looks dire and the challenges insurmountable, there may be a path to success that can be discovered through creative thought and determination.

   Bonnie Hagemann's company, EDA Inc., an executive development firm, could have suffered a tremendous setback when COVID-19 hit. After all, many of her clients were struggling to survive, and the idea of embarking on a new leadership development program was the furthest thing from their minds. So she immediately went to work to set up a new Leadership & Transition Center[14] to provide outplacement and crisis leadership coaching to companies. It's a great example of a leader finding a path forward in turbulent times.

3. **When confronted by a setback, good leaders dust themselves off and carry on.** It's the only way to succeed. Surely not every facet of your execution will go flawlessly! Take difficulties in stride and watch how your people follow suit.

4. **Be open to learning new things.** Sometimes leaders forget how to listen and learn. Don't fall into that trap. You don't have to have all of the answers all of the time.

5. **Welcome those who can coach and teach.** Even world-class athletes have coaches. Surround yourself with people who can make you better.

   As someone who coaches executives and high-potential staffers, I can tell you that many leaders resist seeking coaching support. Some think there's nothing more for them to learn, while others fear being seen as weak or incapable by colleagues. Of course, these are simply excuses. After all, no one knows all there is to know about leadership, and leadership can be a lonely place. That said, leveraging a coach is an idea worth considering. A coach can provide the objective advice and act as an impartial sounding board that is impossible to find anywhere else.

Everyone needs their Yoda!

6. **Communication is the key to engagement.** Your people need to know where you are, what you want, and how you expect them to get there.

7. **Anticipate your response to possible scenarios before they emerge.** Scenario planning enables your organization to anticipate the future and its response to it as predicted situations begin to emerge. This type of planning lessens risk and improves reaction time.

    Consider New Zealand's prime minister Jacinda Ardern's willingness to execute her nation's scenario plan referenced in the first chapter. By anticipating the possibilities of the emergence of a worldwide pandemic, determining New Zealand's response to it, and then executing the plan, she was able to save countless lives and lessen immeasurable suffering of her fellow citizens.

8. **Leadership styles don't discriminate.** Poor leaders come in many shapes and sizes. Regardless of appearance, a poor leader will wreak havoc on any group or organization they are allowed to lead.

9. **Deceitful leaders will destroy all trust within a group.** Once trust deteriorates, the culture becomes cutthroat as each team member begins to fend for themselves—if this happens, eliminate any thoughts of becoming indispensable. It just won't happen.

10. **A vision is best presented as a story that people can relate to.** From an early age, we have all learned to learn through stories. Present your vision as a story that your people can imagine being a part of and you will engage them in the process of making that story a reality.

    Jeroen Lokerse, head of Netherlands Cushman & Wakefield, chose to put his money where his mouth was when developing his post-COVID vision for the workplace. Lokerse built a working office, dubbed the Six Feet Office, that features all of the "back to work" safety measures called out by the World Health Organization,[15] including six-foot desk spacing, one-way foot traffic signage, and transparent protective shields to enable protection should coworkers need to chat at someone's desk.

The Six Feet Office doubles as a showcase for the commercial real estate company's clients—demonstrating what can be done to enable a safe return to work. Indeed, Lokerse has created a "living" vision story for how Cushman & Wakefield returns to work—one that also informs its customers on how they can do the same.

I hope that you find that these tips can be easily adopted and applied to help you lead your organization to indispensability. But remember, like the first tip from this list suggests, you still have to want to do it.

You Have to Want It

Any preemptive change, like driving to indispensability in the marketplace, is about desire. Or, as one senior leader proffered at a recent executive steering committee meeting, "Ya gotta wanna do it." I love this statement: "Ya gotta wanna do it!" It's a straightforward way to summarize an otherwise elegant management philosophy—one that connotes desire, focus, and a commitment to change.

As we close our chapter on the right leadership, let me leave you with five basic leadership principles that I think are the backbone of the "Ya gotta wanna do it" philosophy:

1. **Because leadership is a choice, you must rise to the occasion or get out of the way.**

   If you're not interested in leading the firm to greatness, there are likely hundreds in line behind you who will jump at the chance. So grasp the golden ring and do what you have to do to lead the way, or do everyone a favor and get out of the way so the next person can have their go at it.

   Daniel A. Rykhus is the president and chief executive officer of Raven Industries of Sioux Falls, South Dakota. His company manufactures agricultural spraying equipment, film and sheeting, and technology for use in aerospace and defense. Rykhus serves as a wonderful example of a leader who rose to the occasion during the pandemic, pivoting his firm to the manufacturing of PPE gowns for frontline health-care workers. In July 2020, Raven Industries was awarded a $5 million FEMA contract to deliver critical medical supplies to support the COVID-19 response.[16] Rykhus chose to lead in a time of crisis, and his business was the better for it.

2. **Never rest on your laurels.**

All living entities, like your company, must change and adapt, or they die. It requires investment and tenacity. To keep the level of achievement high and growing in your enterprise, it's important to improve your capabilities for tomorrow even as you continue to focus on execution and performance today. The leadership teams at Amazon and Apple, for example, never rest on their laurels. That's why these companies continue to grow and capture market share. Can you imagine what the world would be like had Steve Jobs decided to ride out into the sunset after launching the Apple II?

If all of your effort goes only into delivering near-term results, you will plateau and risk your competitors speeding past you. Instead, invest your energy every day in building the capabilities you need now and for the future.

3. **Explain the "why."**

It's difficult to teach people to have faith. It's better to provide the "why" so that they can choose to commit to doing the work needed to become indispensable. So fill in the blanks for your team and show them *why* what you're proposing is so compelling and irresistible that they can't help but want to get there with you.

For example, a few years ago, I was working with an insurance software company that was preparing to acquire another software company, which would help them leapfrog their number-one competitor. As part of their change story, I helped them develop a unifying internal communications campaign based on the Transformers film franchise called the "Industry Transformer," which outlined the reasoning and rationale for the acquisition.

The campaign explained why the acquisition would broaden my client's product portfolio, expand its software licensing footprint, and extend its delivery capabilities—all of which helps them achieve their ambitions of becoming the dominant player in the space. Consequently, the response was great, and the staff went out of their way to embrace players from the newly acquired company.

The moral of the story is to do what you have to do to help your people understand the "why" behind the changes that are being pursued. Make it *real*, so they will be willing to do whatever it takes to make it happen.

4. **Dedicate yourself to learning new things.**

We're all "works in progress." No one is the best that they can be. Like I said, all living things must evolve, or they will die. So find people who can make you better.

Reach out to individuals in your professional network who hold, or have held, your role or a similar role in other companies. Share ideas and approaches for solving problems. Joining special interest groups through social media sites like LinkedIn can be an inexpensive place to start.

When coaching, I routinely encourage the executives that I work with to take up new hobbies. This offers at least a couple of advantages down the road. First, it gives them an outlet that takes their mind off the job—something many executives need to maintain good mental and physical health. Second, learning stimulates the mind and creates opportunities for them to expand their decision-making palette by gaining exposure to new things and ideas.

5. **Put insular interests aside for the greater good.**

It may be part of the human condition to be self-serving. But selfishness is a surefire way to fail as a leader of great change. Put your self-interest aside for the greater good of your firm and watch what can be achieved.

For example, John Mackey, CEO of Whole Foods, earned $1 in salary and bonuses in 2016. The company was acquired by Amazon for $13.7 billion in 2017.

By contrast, Chesapeake Energy ousted its former CEO, Aubrey McClendon, after word got out that he allegedly was running a $200 million hedge fund from within company headquarters that speculatively traded in "the same commodities Chesapeake produces."[17] In November 2019, Chesapeake stock dropped to a twenty-five-year low.

Which one of these leaders would you be willing to bust through a brick wall to help?

With that, I hope you agree that the road to indispensability is fraught with challenges. A company doesn't arrive there easily. So you have to want it badly enough to do whatever it takes to get there. Indeed, you have to be the leader who chooses to lead.

To Close

There's no doubt that good leadership is a key to becoming indispensable. Without it, a firm has no chance of becoming the company that their customers prefer. Moreover, as suggested in the previous section, you have to want to do it. You have to be deliberate in becoming the best leader you can be. You owe it to your business, your people, and, just as importantly, yourself to provide exceptional leadership every day.

That said, being an exceptional leader requires that you develop a vibrant vision and wholly socialize it within your organization so that every staff member understands it and sees themselves being successful when it is achieved.

In the next chapter, our Indispensable Agenda calls for us to survey ways of doing the ever-critical vision development and socialization work that makes a company one customers can't live without.

Chapter 2's Indispensable Top Ten List

This chapter is stacked with great content and insight. This list of the top ten takeaways is provided for easy reference. Be sure to take a deeper dive into other key concepts by reviewing the chapter in detail.

1. Exceptional leaders not only possess the requisite honesty and righteousness needed to gain followership, but they emanate the hunger and conviction needed to motivate others to do great things.

2. It requires tremendous courage to stir up the enthusiasm needed to drive an idea as big and expansive as indispensability. It takes even more courage to make all the hard decisions needed to realize that goal.

3. Clearly, leadership and management are strongly related—and managers can certainly lead and leaders can certainly manage—however, the skills required to be exceptional at either one are explicit and pure. We need great leaders to drive a company to indispensability.

4. Organizations tend to take on the personality of their leadership team. Find a firm that is unwavering in its pursuit of indispensability and you'll find leaders who are steady and resolute in their determination to be outstanding in all that they do. Similarly, a company that is unpredictable and inconsistent in its execution tends to have leaders who accept subpar performance.

5. Building a team of passionate leaders begins with proper preparation. Once your people are properly prepared, they can be put into positions that enable them to make decisions that count.

6. You want to be sure to give you and your team the time needed to collaborate, to think, and to decide on the best course of action.

7. Bombarded with questions and issues from every direction, every day, many leaders become extremely reactionary—feeling compelled to immediately answer every question or email that comes their way. Stop!

8. Everyone on the team has an obligation to express his or her dissent. Encourage it because it leads to your best thinking.

9. Leading is a choice—don't squander it. When it comes time to lead, you can rise to the occasion or let someone else take charge. Either way, you live with the consequences of that decision. If you choose to rise to the occasion, do it deliberately and with foresight of action. Don't just "wing" it.

10. Selfishness is a surefire way to fail as a leader of great change. Put your self-interest aside for the greater good of your firm and watch what can be achieved.

The Right Vision

DEVELOPING THE "RIGHT" VISION IS next up on our Indispensable Agenda.

Indispensability takes vision. It needs to be the first plank in your platform—the rock upon which your metaphorical church is built. Without the right vision, it is difficult to inspire your people to do all the work and make all of the changes that they will need to make to reach the pinnacle of indispensability.

Guess what, senior leader? Vision starts with you!

I know it's a lot of responsibility. That said, it's not unusual to feel a bit apprehensive, even fearful, that you lack the insight and inventiveness needed to fit the bill. Stop feeling that way.

It may be true that some seem to be born visionaries. They appear to have an unearthly capacity to anticipate the future. While natural talent helps, it is not a prerequisite for success in crafting a compelling and engaging strategic vision for your business.

In fact, let me offer five simple things that you can do to begin developing your visionary capabilities:

1. **Just keep asking "why not?"** Regularly asking "why not?" acts as a forcing function. You can break through common resistances to new ways of thinking and doing by adopting the convention. Sticking with examining the possibilities enables you to discover

groundbreaking solutions to the most complex challenges facing your firm's path to indispensability.

Elon Musk, CEO of SpaceX and Tesla Motors, has disrupted entire industries by asking the question "why not?" In March of 2019, SpaceX became the first private company to send a human-rated spacecraft to space and the first to autonomously dock a spacecraft on the International Space Station.

According to space.com, "Musk believes that a fully (and rapidly) reusable rocket is the key to dramatically reducing the cost of spaceflight. The company has already shown it can reuse the most expensive portion of the rocket—the first stage—but would like to reuse much more, essentially making fuel the only major expense."[1]

2. **Flex your imagination muscles.** Reimagining how the work of your business can be accomplished may be a pathway to the future for you. It is through such considerations that visionary thinking happens. Taking time to imagine the possibilities helps reveal the path to great advancement.

   Google's parent company, Alphabet, provides a great example of imagination at work with its introduction of Wing—a service that delivers commercial goods to residences via drone.

   Last year, Montgomery County Public Schools in Virginia were closed due to the coronavirus and students couldn't visit the library, making it difficult for them to keep up with their reading. So school librarian Kelly Passek decided to use Wing as a means of delivering library books to schoolchildren.

   Passek explained, "We are thrilled for this opportunity to have a really unique way to deliver resources to our students and do it practically on demand."[2]

   Alphabet clearly has innovation in its DNA, so it's no wonder that its leadership team came forward with an idea for reimagining home delivery.

3. **Mix contrasting ideas into your thinking.** The act of connecting disparate thoughts and theories together to produce new and

trailblazing perspectives is what vision-setting is all about. The practice feeds innovative thinking, which is a fundamental characteristic of truly visionary leaders.

Consider the case of Casper CEO Philip Krim, who, along with his partners, completely reimagined the process of buying and delivering a bed by designing a high-quality, multilayer foam mattress that could be squeezed into a three-and-a-half-foot tall box and shipped to your door.

Together, Krim and his associates saw a way to combine mattress-buying (typically done through brick-and-mortar stores) with online e-tailing by solving the shipping problem through innovative design and packaging.

When celebrity Kylie Jenner showed off her "unboxing" pictures on Instagram, the company knew it had arrived, prompting Neil Parikh, one of Casper's cofounders, to say, "Oh my God, when Kylie Jenner posted about Casper I think it broke our website!"[3]

4. **Become synergistic.** As the old adage suggests, two brains are better than one! Pull ideas and concepts from like-minded people. Synergistic thinking will unearth the insights and perspectives needed to round out your vision. It can provide the means to better define a robust and compelling case for becoming indispensable.

   Disney's Bob Iger is a master at seeking and acting upon synergies. While at the helm, he has driven the acquisition of trailblazing animation studio Pixar, Marvel Entertainment, and the Star Wars franchise—which reinvigorated the old and well-established Disney brand and made it new again.

   However, his acquisition of 21st Century Fox, the largest deal ever in the entertainment industry, is Iger's crowning achievement. With this content added to the portfolio, he has positioned Disney+ to compete in the world of streaming video-on-demand services with the likes of Netflix and Amazon.

   Finding and leveraging synergies is one of the ways great companies, like Disney, become indispensable.

5. **Develop customer empathy.** Seeing the business from an outsider's point of view is always illuminating. The practice of putting yourself in the customer's shoes and imagining what it must
be like to do business with you can help identify opportunities for
improvement within your company. It can force the reexamination
of your "sacred cows." It can open you up to discover the best ways
to delight your customers.

Take Marriott, for instance. CEO Arne Sorenson has placed
a renewed emphasis on the customer experience. By looking at
Marriott through the lens of the guest, the hotelier has introduced
a whole slew of new benefits through its "Bonvoy Moments" program for brand loyalists, including using points to pay for experiences like private cooking lessons with famous chefs, VIP concert
tickets, and trips on private yachts.

For added convenience, guests can use the Marriott app to communicate directly with hotels about their preferences before and
during their stays and use their smartphones as room keys at hundreds of Marriott properties.

His commitment to enriching the customer experience through
innovative thinking is one of the reasons that *Chief Executive Magazine* named him the 2019 CEO of the year.[4]

It is true that not everyone is a natural-born visionary. However, with
work and perseverance, you can develop the skills needed to become better at anticipating the future—an attribute that can help you become the
type of leader who can inspire greatness and lead your organization to
unprecedented heights of indispensability. Once you have some ideas for
where you want to lead your organization, it's time to share them with
other leaders within the enterprise and gain their thoughts in further
shaping them.

Shaping Your Vision

It takes more than *cult of personality* to drive your vision throughout an enterprise. You need buy-in and help from the rest of the management team. Here are some steps to take to share and solicit input from other leaders within the business:

1. **Engage other senior leaders** in a conversation about where you should, as a team, collectively bring the organization. Solicit their ideas regarding direction and change. Compel them to identify the biggest challenges confronting the business and work with them to identify possible solutions. These conversations will enable you to give your ideas a "dry run" before taking it to the people.

   A few years back, Jeffrey Glazer, then the CEO of the Insurance Division of LexisNexis' Risk Solutions Group, engaged me to help him and his team craft a vision story for his division. The very first thing we did was schedule and conduct a series of interviews with each of his top leaders. The idea was to gain a perspective from each executive on what they saw as opportunities for the future and how they would like to see the business operate under their leadership.

   The approach proved invaluable. While there was great consistency among the team concerning strategic direction, each leader had added something unique and special when offering their point of view about how they would like to see the business operate. Those nuggets became major themes in the resulting vision that we created for the business.

2. **Gain assistance and input from middle management and supervisory staff** through dedicated workshops that provide a platform for them to offer insight and opinion about what they see as important areas of focus for them. You will want to be sure that your vision addresses any themes that emerge from these workshops. After all, it is your middle layer of leaders who make change

happen within your daily operations. If they see that you hear them, they will begin to buy into your ideas for the future.

This approach proved worthwhile at LexisNexis. Once we gained executive insight from Glazer's leadership team, we went on to solicit input from the middle management layer of the division. Several cross-functional workshops were held. Special attention was paid to testing some of the ideas brought out in the executive interviews. This technique enabled us to extend and refine the thinking while enabling the middle management team to gain a sense of ownership of the vision story.

3. **Survey the execution layer of the enterprise** so to gain a ground-level perspective from the people doing the work in the trenches. This can be accomplished through the administration of online survey instruments and informal functional-level huddles among frontline staff.

Both of these ideas were used at LexisNexis. We ran several shorter meetings with supervisors, discussing each of the themes that would be covered in the vision story. The dialogue from those informal huddles helped better shape what needed to be covered in the vision story in order to resonate with line personnel. Additionally, an online survey went out to staff to solicit reactions to the key ideas that were emerging through the various interviews, workshops, and huddles.

4. **Synthesize the results** and identify common issues and ideas for change. These should be used to cultivate the content of your vision. Think of them as potential section headings in a vision story.

This exercise was stress-free at LexisNexis. The themes identified through the executive interviewing process were vetted extremely well in the middle management workshops, supervisory-level huddles, and workforce surveying. All we had to do was determine the details to be highlighted within each theme to make the vision story easy to follow and understand.

5. **Outline the story that you want to tell.** Make your vision come alive by identifying what you want to say about all of the input and

insights that you have cultivated. Take it all in and then begin to determine how you can construct a great story about where you want to bring the company.

LexisNexis landed on ideas related to market focus, speed, culture, quality, and talent, among other things. Their resulting vision story took the form of a magazine, highlighted by feature articles written by each of the senior leaders. In turn, each of those articles focused on one of the key strategic themes.

It was a creative and an effective way to articulate the vision while demonstrating to staff the executive team's commitment to achieving it.

Why a Story?

From the time that we are very young, stories help us learn about the world around us. Stories inform our thinking about what is right and wrong. They reinforce the cultural norms and societal values of the places where we live. Indeed, the stories that we are told—and read— continue to enlighten and reshape our thinking throughout the rest of our lives. In fact, nearly two-thirds of our daily conversations are story-centered.[5]

This is why I believe top leaders need to create vibrant and captivating vision stories as a means to inform and inspire the people who hear and read them. In fact, LexisNexis used its vision story as part of the firm's sales and marketing, often using the magazine as a "leave behind" in sales meetings.

What's more, it is part of the human condition to search for understanding and to want to be part of something bigger than ourselves. These desires are the reasons that we form communities, join religious communities, and root for sports teams. It is the reason we get up in the morning.

As business leaders, don't we owe our people that little "extra something" that serves to enlighten, engage, and inspire them? Given the huge amount of time that people dedicate to their jobs, it only makes sense for us to feed some of their need to belong by providing a solid call to action that they can believe in. If we can do that, we will garner our people's best effort.

Shortly after the vision story came out at LexisNexis, the company closed one of its largest software deals ever with Allstate Insurance. While I'm not claiming that the deal came together because the firm had a terrific vision story, I am suggesting that nothing can convey the kind of call to action needed to close your next *big deal* better than a good story!

Let the Writing Begin

To be clear, I'm not recommending that you invest time in developing the same tired and uninspired vision statements that appear on company websites or are printed on banners strung from company rafters.

You know the ones I'm writing about: "We ignite opportunity by setting the world in motion" or "To provide access to the world's information in one click."

These kinds of company visions (taken from actual companies) are a dime a dozen. They are nice slogans—cute and amusing catchphrases, but not particularly inspiring. They don't describe the company or what it's like to be part of the organization. They don't serve to distinguish a specific enterprise from its competitors because they can apply to any company within the industry. Your vision should be much more than slogans and catchphrases.

You want to construct a vision story so compelling and vivid that the average working professional wants to be part of it. To accomplish this, the story must have the necessary depth and detail to capture one's imagination. It should include your overarching ideas refined by the thoughts and suggestions gained through the conversations, workshops, and survey information that was gathered from your leaders and personnel.

Above all else, it must be enlightening and riveting, or your people won't get revved up about achieving it.

When we developed the vision story for GDLS, for example, we made sure that staff could relate to the messages that it contained by including pictures and quotes from employees in the vision story publication.

Seeing colleagues and reading their comments espousing the virtues of the company's vision made the vision story really "pop" for company personnel.

Make It Thought-Provoking*

People must be able to identify with what is being proffered within your vision story. They need to be able to see themselves working and being successful within the company that your story describes. Make it so thought-provoking that a staff member will not be satisfied working at any other place in the world.

Typically fifteen to twenty pages in length, the story must be a vast and detailed discussion of what an organization is to *become* in order to be indispensable. It should be revolutionary in its tone and loose and graceful in its organization. Be sure to write in a way that suggests that the organization has already arrived at its vision for the future by imagining the possibilities that exist today.

Most of the vision stories that I have worked on with my clients begin with a strong statement of the financial goal. For instance, a $10 billion health insurance company may have a vision story that starts with "We have become a $10 billion company over the past five years by helping people achieve health and financial security through the provision of easy access to safe, cost-effective, high-quality health care and protecting their finances against health-related risks."

In other words, the goal is to become a $10 billion company in five years. However, the vision story presents it to the reader as if the firm has already achieved it.

Past the financial goal, the vision story has to give staff additional details that they need to know in order to get behind its achievement. Ideas related to the size of the company should be part of the discussion. It distinguishes the target among options (i.e., small and growing, midsize and specialized, large and dominating, etc.). These kinds of data are important because people need to identify with the size and goals of the firms for which they work in order to give the organization their best effort.

---

*   The following section is based on my piece, "Strategic Visioning" published on management-issues.com, July 27, 2009.

Here are more dimensions of the business that should be presented in the vision story:

Leadership Style	Diversity and Inclusion
Customer Demographics	Culture
Growth Strategies	Product/Service Sets
Service Delivery	Product Distribution
Brand Value	New Business Partnerships
Operating Model	Organizational Structure
Talent and Workforce	Process Innovations
Composition	Quality Frameworks
Communication	Project Portfolios
Infrastructure	Governance Frameworks

This is not to say that the vision story specifies, in gory detail, the steps taken to get there. Rather, it simply characterizes what has been targeted to be achieved within each of these facets of the business.

For example, the following passage, from an actual vision story developed just as the firm was getting back to work after the pandemic temporarily shuttered the business, was used to describe the "Workforce Composition" topic:

> By fostering an open and honest relationship with staff during the COVID-19 shutdown, a responsive, more flexible workforce is in place. Effective cross-training and education programs have been instituted as well. This allows the company to respond rapidly to workflow peaks and valleys.
>
> Highly complex processes are now performed directly by front-line associates with an "If I can do it, I will!" mentality broadly sweeping across the company.
>
> Training efforts have broadened their focus from job-specific development to ones where overall process knowledge, interpersonal skills, leadership development, methodology practices, management skills, and succession planning are provided.

Notice that there is a lot of detail describing the resultant work setting that has been instituted within this enterprise. There is little information about how the workforce flexibility was achieved, and there is nothing about specific training plans or how demand and capacity are managed in order to institute the flexible workforce. Instead, the passage purely states that the company now possesses these attributes.

As mentioned, most vision stories are fifteen to twenty pages in length. Once it's in good shape, it's time to consider how it will be distributed. It is absolutely essential that you get the story out and socialized across the entire organization. From the floor sweepers to the boardroom, everyone in the enterprise needs to understand and embrace the vision story.

Socializing the Story across the Enterprise

Interestingly, I have helped clients craft stories in a wide variety of ways over the years. I've helped build vision stories in storyboard form much like a graphic novel. I have been asked, as in the LexisNexis example discussed earlier, to organize vision stories into a series of articles that can be combined and published as one would produce a magazine.

I have even helped a senior leadership team at Jewelers Mutual in Neenah, Wisconsin, deliver their vision story to their personnel in an aircraft hangar. It was a trade-show setting containing several booths (or stations), each featuring a top leader from the management team discussing a specific element of the vision story. People got the whole story by visiting each station.

From experience, I can tell you that it is wise to make the distribution of your vision story a multimedia affair. People learn and retain information in many different ways. You simply improve the odds of everyone understanding the story by delivering it in different forms.

We used a multiprong approach for story distribution when working with Connecticut's Department of Revenue Services too. Their story was published as a document that was sent to all staff. This was followed by the broadcasting of a video that featured then commissioner Kevin Sullivan presenting the highlights of the vision story from his desk in the executive suite. The roll-out was capped off by a series of "fireside chats," which enabled staff members to gather in small groups with Sullivan to discuss aspects of the story. This commitment to establishing understanding among agency staffers went a long way to gain their buy-in.

Of course, once you determine the media and means of distribution, be sure to properly target your audiences.

Targeting Each Audience

As referenced earlier in the chapter, every organization has at least three different audiences that need to be involved with vision development—the top, the middle, and the lower layers of the organization. These same groups must be engaged when rolling out the finished vision story product(s).

Think of your business as a pyramid divided into three layers. The top layer of the pyramid is comprised of the top leaders. These are the people responsible for setting strategic direction and guiding the enterprise toward its future. While certainly concerned with quarterly performance, the leaders at the top of the pyramid must also have a forward-looking, "Where will we be in five years?" kind of mind-set. They need to envision what indispensable looks like inside the enterprise.

When working with Mitsui Sumitomo Insurance on their U.S. operations vision story, for example, we took the time to provide each executive with a personalized "cheat sheet" of sorts that summarized the potential for them when the vision is achieved. As you might imagine, the sales executive's summary described increased revenue, the claims executive's spelled out seamless claims adjudication, while underwriting's addressed faster, error-free risk assessment. These cheat sheets served us well by maintaining leadership buy-in while providing the leadership team with the fodder that they would need to convince their staffs of the potential that the vision offered each of them.

As the name implies, the middle layer of the pyramid is comprised of the middle management of the organization. These people must be able to interpret the strategic direction set forth by the senior leaders and translate it into actions that the units that report to them can understand and act on. While these managers certainly care about strategy, their primary focus is the current year. Can we do what we need this year to reach our goals and objectives? Be sure to tell the story in a way that the middle layer can interpret and translate your intent into action for their people.

Particular attention was paid to this at General Dynamics. The division's president at the time, Gary Whited, spent countless hours promoting and discussing the vision story with his directors as it was being rolled out. In fact, he hosted a three-day off-site gathering for fifty of his next-level leaders so that they could fully grasp and internalize the essence of the story and discern what it meant to each of them.

Finally, the lower layer of the pyramid is comprised of supervisors and the rank and file. This layer is responsible for execution. Their time horizon is much different from that of their middle managers and top leaders. Their point of reference is today. Can we do the work that must be done today, on time and on budget? Additionally, they inherently understand that they will suffer the consequences of poor performance if they don't execute as expected. So be sure to present the vision story in a way that informs how the lower layer will execute and get the job done.

When working with The Hartford on this, we went so far as to produce and distribute a storyboard placemat that summarized, in graphic form, the key elements of the vision story. The storyboard highlighted the use of digital technology to improve claim handling. It showed how customer support could be boosted via chatbots. It even had a frame depicting actuaries using enriched data analytics to improve product pricing. The technique was an effective way to help staff professionals better understand how vision achievement would make their job easier to perform.

Before we wrap up our discussion about establishing the right vision for becoming indispensable, let me offer one last tip: *focus on the middle!*

The Middle Layer Will Make or Break You

It is my belief that the middle management team makes or breaks strategic execution!

As mentioned, they're the ones who must interpret the strategies and translate them into something that is actionable by the *troops in the trenches*. If they fail to do this well, the organization falters, resources are squandered, and unfortunately, many times heads roll. Therefore, the vision story must be delivered to them in a way that encourages their understanding and buy-in.

Here are three simple guidelines that will help you get them on board (and, by doing so, improve your chances for success in realizing your vision of becoming indispensable to your customers):

1. **Talk and teach:** Think about it—you are asking your midtier managers to act as teachers. Likewise, to teach well, they must first understand. So commit to establishing the understanding that they'll need to help the rest of your organization grasp and commit to your vision. Do all that you can to help them comprehend all of the content and nuances of those strategic elements of the story. Help them by outlining specific actions that they can take immediately to get the ball rolling.

The off-site meeting hosted by Gary Whited at General Dynamics, as referenced earlier, serves as a good example of this in action. Several small group break-out sessions underpinned the three-day meeting. These provided opportunities for directors to talk to each other about implications of the vision and determine ways to work together to achieve its intent.

2. **Jump-start the translation:** Don't leave it up to your middle management to determine how they will go about communicating what the pursuit of indispensability really means to the people whom they manage. Instead, take the time to think about all of the implications and likely actions that you would need to tackle in helping

the organization reimagine the way work is done within the enterprise. Give them a template to use to drive the message down into the organization.

Along with the executive cheat sheets described earlier, we developed an entire roll-out briefing package at Mitsui Sumitomo Insurance. It enabled middle managers to cascade the vision messaging deeper into the company. It enabled the middle layer to have meaningful conversations with their staff members about the "wherefores and the whys" contained in the vision story, which led to deeper understanding and acceptance of the insurer's strategic vision.

3. **Coordinate the delivery:** Once you equip your managers with the requisite knowledge and communication content, they can begin to flow the message throughout the rest of the organization. However, they may not do this in a disciplined and rigorous way. So be sure to coordinate the sharing of the information by establishing a roll-out schedule that details when the managers should deliver strategic messaging to their teams.

We followed a simple but effective roll-out schedule at LexisNexis. First, the vision magazine was mailed to each staff member. Two weeks after the mailing, we held a conference that enabled staff to hear aspirational messages from each member of the executive team about the division's vision for the future. Two weeks after the conference, departmental meetings were held, and area managers briefed their teams using the presentation packages that we prepared for them.

Don't Forget Digital When Crafting Your Future Vision

Today's digital capabilities offer great promise. When constructing your vision story, be sure to consider how those enhanced capabilities will impact the future of your business.

That's exactly what retailer JustFab Inc. did when developing their vision for changing the shopping experience.

JustFab Inc.'s co-CEOs, Don Ressler and Adam Goldenberg, launched Fabletics with Kate Hudson in 2013 after they saw a gap in the activewear marketplace. The team saw service aided by technology and an empowered workforce as a key to success. Prior to the COVID-19 outbreak, retail associates carried touch-screen devices (off-the-shelf iPod Touch units running the company's software) around the store. An associate can bring up the account of a VIP customer, make recommendations, open a virtual shopping cart, and handle the entire interaction.

According to the retailer's chief operating officer Anton von Rueden, "You feel really empowered with this thing, because you can walk up to any customer in the store and solve every single one of their problems. . . . You can do exchanges, returns, go online to order items not in the store. There aren't people who just do replenishment on the racks. There aren't people who just do checkout. Basically every store associate can do every process—and they do."[6]

It seems Fabletics has blurred the lines of traditional retailer staff roles and improved the customer experience as a result.

It's a good thing that they had already begun to absorb the digital learning curve when the pandemic hit. Indeed, the e-tailer was able to pivot and create an online shopping experience that mimics their in-store one, providing VIP members the same kind of care and convenience that they've grown accustomed to when shopping at Fabletics.

Consider how you can fold digital capabilities into your vision story too. It may, as in the case of Fabletics, come to serve you well in the future.

Acknowledge the Changes Forced by the Pandemic

It's an understatement to say that the COVID-19 pandemic has forever changed the way work is done. That said, it's important that your vision story reflects some of the changes that you made at its onset, and intend to keep going-forward, like:

- The traditional organizational structure has been adjusted to accommodate remote personnel. Current command and control structures have been updated to allow greater flexibility in managing personnel and monitoring their performance.
- Management's roles have changed in this more flexible work environment as well. Managers are prepared to become less directive and to fine-tune the coaching skills that are needed to motivate geographically dispersed personnel.
- Processes have been reengineered, independent of current organizational boundaries, with an emphasis placed on performing the "whole job" instead of only specific pieces.
- Jobs have been redefined too. All attendant responsibilities and commitments related to performing the "whole job" are now folded into job specifications.
- The need for training every employee in the fundamentals of a firm's business processes has been amplified as a result of working remotely. Personnel have come to understand that business processes are virtual by nature and that specifying where work is performed is far less important than getting the work done right the first time.

Indeed, including these kinds of recent business adjustments are important items to reflect in your future vision story. Of course, they're not all that you should consider including in that story.

Other Ideas to Consider Including in Your Vision Story

Before we wrap up our vision story discussion, I thought it worthwhile to take a moment to consider some other ideas to make your vision story "pop."

For example, your vision story could do the following:

1. **Describe leaders who often talk about the greater purpose of the organization.** This could attract different talent to your

organization, and this talent may bring fresh ideas into play that could lead to indispensability.

2. **Define a workplace where leaders preach a "Do your job" mentality.** This could motivate staff to feel duty-bound to do their jobs at the highest level so as not to let their teammates down. This kind of workforce is a characteristic of an indispensable business.

3. **Highlight how smart risk-taking is encouraged.** This could encourage leaders to venture out of their comfort zones and bring about indispensability.

4. **Underscore that "doing good" is a recognized value of the organization.** This will disrupt the status quo and could bring about indispensability.

5. **Characterize the work environment as being fully aligned with the business strategy.** This shift could make you the *provider of choice* in your market.

6. **Outline the ways that personnel embrace and accept change.** This new adaptability may motivate new behaviors among staffers, and your company culture will shift, enabling indispensability.

7. **Sketch out how intense customer focus leads to growth.** This orientation may set the path for becoming indispensable.

8. **Discuss the creation of an organization that promotes the betterment of society through its work within it.** People may begin to take more pride in the organization and do what needs to be done for it to become indispensable.

These are some of the ideas that can be used to round out your vision story and give it a unique personality.

Yes, Your Company Has a Personality Too!

As a person who has worked with countless leadership teams in developing and crafting their vision stories, I often wonder just how the resulting vision is being perceived by those we intend to inform and motivate. I often wonder what the persona, or personality, is of the organization that we've just described through our work.

To scratch that itch, my team at General Dynamics and I put their vision story to the test.

We used IBM Watson's Personality Insights,[7] which applies linguistic analytics and personality theory based on the "Big Five" personality traits (i.e., extroversion, agreeableness, openness, conscientiousness, and neuroticism) to infer attributes from a person's writing sample.

We fed the recently completed vision story to Watson so that it could report on the personality of the organization that we just described in the story. Since the vision story was developed by multiple people who each wrote specific sections of the story, we felt the findings produced would reflect the company's personality and not that of the specific authors.

The experiment did not disappoint—the detailed analysis and data analytics provided this personality summary about the vision at the company:

> You are imaginative and motivated.
>
> You are assertive. You have a tendency to take the lead in most situations, and you are seen as a natural leader. You are energetic. You revel in a fast-paced environment. And you are trusting of others. You expect people to deliver their best effort.
>
> You are driven to overcome obstacles.
>
> You are notably unconcerned with tradition. And you are more interested in charting your own course than following what others have done.
>
> You opt for activities that serve a greater purpose.

This analysis means that if this client's future company were a person, that person would have, among others, these characteristics: imagination, drive, high trust, pioneering spirit, and an interest in serving a greater purpose—the very same characteristics that make companies indispensable.

Good news and validation are provided by this insight. The good news is that, together with the General Dynamics team, the vision story constructed conveys exactly the tone and sentiment that was intended. The validation that the analysis provided suggests that the necessary work required to transform the company appears to be a worthwhile endeavor.

Of course, this kind of analysis is not the be-all and end-all of vision work. At the end of the day, the tool that we used is a free demo product intended to get firms interested in licensing software. However, this kind of analysis provides insights and perspectives that an organization may not have gathered otherwise—insights about how its vision might be perceived by staffers and insights about how the business might be perceived by customers once it is transformed.

I believe that it is a good idea to apply personality theory in strategic planning and vision work. After all, every organization is a unique and living thing by virtue of the fact that each is shaped by the unique group of people who comprise it. I think that combining these disciplines has groundbreaking potential. I am convinced that it will lead to meaningful outcomes for any business interested in disrupting its industry and becoming indispensable.

To Close

By heralding a vision story that accentuates sound fundamentals yet unveils a future that people want to be part of, businesses can establish a strategic platform from which to introduce new programs and extend existing ones that position them to be nimble and quick while still growing and evolving into broader-reaching and more profitable organizations.

Indeed, vision storytelling is an essential part of change management. It provides an attractive framework for setting direction and managing change, and more notably, it presents an opportunity to convey your vision to the masses so that they can understand and buy into your pursuit of making the company indispensable.

Regardless of the form that the story takes, vision stories help leadership teams convey a convincing case for change. These stories play a key role in describing why indispensability is an essential goal.

They set boundaries on strategic choices and serve as a terrific screen for selecting new projects and programs for the organization to prioritize and execute. Vision stories set a tone and direction that a vision statement just cannot do!

They tell the story of how an organization will become indispensable.

Next, let's look at the culture shift needed to support the journey. Building the "right" culture is, after all, next on our agenda.

Chapter 3's Indispensable Top Ten List

This chapter is stacked with great content and insight. This list of the top ten takeaways is provided for easy reference. Be sure to take a deeper dive into other key concepts by reviewing the chapter in detail.

1. Top leaders must create vibrant and captivating vision stories as a means to inform and inspire their people and stakeholders.
2. Indeed, indispensability takes vision. Without the right vision, it is difficult to inspire your people to do all the work and make all of the changes needed to reach the pinnacle of indispensability.
3. People must be able to identify with what is being proffered within your vision story. They need to be able to see themselves working and being successful within the company that your story describes. Make it so thought-provoking and riveting that a staff member will not be satisfied working anywhere else.
4. It takes more than cult of personality to drive your vision throughout an enterprise. You need buy-in and help from the rest of the management team.
5. Every organization has at least three different audiences to involve with vision development—the top, the middle, and the lower layers of the organization. The best vision stories target all three audiences.
6. The middle management team makes or breaks strategic execution. They're the ones who must interpret the strategies and translate them into something that is actionable by the rank and file. If they fail to do this well, the organization falters, resources are squandered, and unfortunately, many times heads roll. Therefore,

the vision story must be delivered to them in a way that inspires buy-in.

7. Vision stories can take a wide variety of forms from graphic novels to videos to professionally produced magazines—use the formats that work best for you.

8. Today's digital capabilities offer great promise. When crafting your vision story, be sure to consider how those enhanced capabilities will impact the future of your business.

9. It is a good idea to apply personality theory in your vision-shaping work. After all, every organization is a unique and living thing by virtue of the fact that each is shaped by the unique group of people who comprise it—sculpt your vision in support of the personality of your business.

10. By heralding a vision story that accentuates sound fundamentals yet unveils a future that people want to be part of, businesses can establish a strategic platform from which to introduce new programs and extend existing ones, which positions companies to become indispensable.

The Right Culture

IF YOU WANT TO BE indispensable, you need the right culture. Period. End of sentence. It is for this reason that developing the "right" culture is our next Indispensable Agenda item.

Not convinced that culture is important? Unclear if it's worth the effort to transform yours? The return on investment not obvious enough for you? No problem. Just answer a few questions for me[*]:

1. **What's the value of strategic alignment?** Getting your culture aligned with where you want to take your business is absolutely critical to achieving your vision for the future. After all, you won't realize the vision if your company culture can't support it.
2. **What's the value of improved teamwork?** Getting your people to work as one is instrumental to business success. Your culture must be set up to do that. If it isn't, your performance will undoubtedly suffer.
3. **What's the value of a high-trust work setting?** All good things are based on trust. If your culture is built on trust, your business is well-positioned to overcome all of the obstacles that will confront it in its journey to strategic accomplishment.
4. **What's the value of improved communication?** Communication is the centerpiece of every business. Outward communication drives prospective customers to your door and supports them once

---

[*] This section is based on my Inc.com article: "The ROI of Culture Transformation," August 24, 2017.

they've made the choice to become actual customers. Internal communication keeps your people informed so that they can perform at their best. Your culture better support transparent communication; if it doesn't, it may be time to invest in cultural transformation.

5. **What's the value of improved customer intimacy?** It's tough to stay in business without satisfied customers! Your culture should be built around understanding their needs and wants and then delivering impeccable service so that you become the provider of choice.

6. **What's the value of high resiliency?** Running a successful business is a rough and tumble undertaking. Your company culture will determine its ability to withstand and overcome adversity.

7. **What's the value of being a talent magnet?** You want exceptional people? Build a company culture that makes you the *employer of choice*. Great cultures attract great talent. Be sure your culture is outstanding.

8. **What's the value of greater innovation?** Your products and services better be amazing if you intend to continue to grow your business. Here's where innovation comes in. By creating a culture that continuously innovates, you improve your ability to be amazing.

What's the value of all of this to your organization? I hope that you've quickly proven to yourself that investing in culture transformation is perhaps the best thing that you can do to become an indispensable enterprise.

Indeed, company culture is the foundation of every business because it determines how people behave. If you optimize the culture and ensure its alignment with the achievement of your strategic objectives, your business performance will improve. Place a value on that and compare it to the cost of cultural transformation and you'll have an ROI that makes the case to invest in culture transformation. It's really that simple!

True Cultural Transformation Is Serious Business

With so much written about all of the fab cultures spawned by Silicon Valley darlings like Google and Pixar, one would be led to believe that you have to install a skateboard park right in the middle of your executive suite in order to compete. Nothing could be further from the truth!

Consider the impact that the pandemic has had on the work setting. The open concept, so popular in modern office settings, has had to be replaced with Plexiglas barriers and foot-traffic-routing signage to improve employee health and safety. Quite a hit to the sleep-pod aesthetic popularized by the high-tech crowd.

The fact is, corporate culture is no laughing matter, and it must be fashioned in a very deliberate way to avoid all kinds of problematic consequences, like these:

1. **Your business routinely falls short of its goals.** *Underperformance* is a key indicator that "Rome is burning" within your business. Lackluster performance can suggest a lack of understanding, ability, or interest among staff to do better—and those characteristics suggest that your company culture needs to be deliberately improved.

   Microsoft is a prime example of a firm that recognizes the need for a culture overhaul as it continues to struggle to maintain its dominance in the ever-changing software marketplace.

   CEO Satya Nadella has taken aim on shifting the culture by breaking up the Windows and Devices Group, flattening the organization structure, eliminating the company's stack-ranking employee review system (stack ranking is a system in which employees are compared against each other instead of against their own goals), and introducing diversity goals to the management compensation program.[1]

   The hope is that these measures will help revitalize a business that seems to have stalled a bit in recent years.

2. **Your people don't demonstrate a strong commitment to the firm.** Weak *company affiliation* is reflected in high employee turnover,

low energy, and less than stellar net promoter scores. It also indicates a cultural weakness that hurts the retention of your best and brightest while negatively impacting your company's performance.

To be sure, it is impossible to be indispensable if your company is a perennial member of a "Worst Company to Work For" list. Take Hertz, for example. According to 24/7 Wall St., who since 2012 has annually analyzed employee reviews at jobs and career community site Glassdoor to produce the list, "Florida-based rental car company Hertz has some of the most dissatisfied employees of any large American company. Employee reviews on Glassdoor regularly complain about the company's culture and values as well as its senior management. From the reviews, company CEO Kathryn Marinello has a 50% approval rating. Meanwhile, Pam Nicholson, the CEO of Enterprise, one of Hertz's major competitors, enjoys an 89% approval rating."[2]

Perhaps this partially explains why Hertz filed for bankruptcy last May after laying off sixteen thousand employees due to the impact of the pandemic on its business. However, Hertz has made the list more than once. Clearly, there are opportunities for improvement in Hertz's company culture.

3. **Your people don't trust their leaders.** A mistrust of *leadership and management* can present itself in many ways, including staff regularly questioning management's motivations, behaviors, and practices. High mistrust indicates a company culture in need of repair.

Uber is a company that just might have a huge culture problem. In June 2017, Travis Kalanick stepped down as Uber's CEO because of the firm's notoriously unrestrained "bro" culture. By year's end, Kalanick's replacement and current CEO, Dara Khosrowshahi, was wrestling through the fallout from allegations by the *Wall Street Journal*[3] that he knew about a data breach that put fifty-seven million Uber customer's personal and financial information at risk for months before he took the initiative to notify affected customers.

How can anyone at Uber trust its leadership? It is little wonder that there have been countless reports since about Uber's toxic work environment.

4. **Your people can't connect "what they do" to business results.** A lack of *strategic alignment and staff connection*, as demonstrated by an undercurrent of doubt and misunderstanding about company direction among staffers, points to a lack of communication. Poor communication is a productivity killer.

How do you think Toyota staff feels about *connection* and being heard when, as a recent article in *Forbes* reports, their warnings to their CEO about critical safety issues went unnoticed? "More than three years before Toyota faced massive safety issues and recalls, employees wrote a memo to the CEO warning him that cost-cutting measures were impacting the safety of the cars. Employees even connected early issues with acceleration and brake systems to five deaths and used that to warn executives, but the cries went unnoticed and more than 8 million cars were recalled."[4]

A tough lesson in the importance of forging a culture of listening.

5. **Your people describe working in silos (and you don't own a farm!).** A lack of *collaboration and teamwork* among staff and work units suggests an organization in need of cultural repair. After all, the best results come from the "we," not the "I."

General Motors' faulty ignition switch debacle of 2014, where more than twenty million vehicles were recalled after thirteen deaths and countless injuries were reported, serves as a solid example of what can happen to a company that suffers from a "siloed culture."

An internal probe by former federal prosecutor Anton Valukas revealed that organizational silos—or the lack of interdepartmental communication between employees—were a contributing factor to the faulty part not being recognized as a potential consumer safety problem.[5]

GM is not the only large company wrestling with the issue of silos getting in the way of good business—it is a deep-rooted cultural challenge for many organizations and is one that you should look out for on your pursuit of indispensability.

6. **Your people don't feel that they have what they need to perform at their best.** Staff must be enabled to get their jobs done. *Enablement* comes from having the tools, resources, and freedom required to reinvent the way work is performed. Often overlooked as a cultural element, a lack of enablement can make or break a corporate culture.

    In February 2019, Southwest Airlines grounded more than forty of its planes, wreaking all kinds of havoc throughout their airline system with excessive flight delays and cancelations. The airline blamed the union for slowing work; the union complained that union members were working overtime but lacked the resources to get the work done.[6]

    This example demonstrates that even a company like Southwest, which is known for its terrific work environment, can come up short when it comes to culture, which can have an adverse effect on a firm's ability to remain indispensable in the hearts and minds of its customers.

7. **Your people don't feel like they "own" the results.** Empowering people to use their own free will to exceed all expectations can enhance their sense of ownership and responsibility. Many leaders underestimate the importance of empowerment in their cultures—don't become one of them!

    Hubspot, the CRM software platform company, has about 3,200 employees in nine offices around the world. It believes that happy employees do the best work, wherever and whenever they like to work. And so staff members can work remotely, keep non-traditional hours, and use unlimited vacation to create the work setting that works for them.

    This kind of empowerment may sound a bit radical, even by today's standards; however, the proof is in the pudding. In November 2019, the company reported a 32 percent increase in total revenue from the year prior[7] and, by all accounts, has done just fine in weathering the COVID-19 crisis.

8. **Your people grumble about the lack of positive feedback.**
The absence of *feedback and recognition* within an organization suggests that it is a tough place to work. Tough places of work are often the ones riddled with deep-rooted culture challenges that, if left unchecked, can lead to their total collapse. Data show that places that provide their staff with feedback simply perform better.

For instance, Gallup, the global analytics firm, found the following in a recent study:[8]

- Employees who received feedback had 14.9 percent lower turnover rates than those who received no feedback.
- Teams with managers who received regular feedback showed 12.5 percent greater productivity than teams with managers who received no feedback.
- Similarly, profit centers with managers who received feedback showed 8.9 percent greater profitability than profit centers in which the manager received no feedback.

Clearly, feedback counts!

9. **Your people are critical of the lack of opportunity that exists in the firm.** Career stagnation is often a characteristic of an organization that lacks a commitment to *learning and development*. Personnel feel handcuffed in current roles and can't move up because they're not presented with the opportunities needed to develop the skills required to advance.

When IBM audited its employee skills five years ago, for example, only about a third of its employees had the skills needed by the company to support its clients. IBM realized it needed to "skill up" if it hoped to continue to compete. In response, they began a vigorous training program, dedicating about $500,000 per year to employee education, ensuring that every staff member received at least sixty hours of education annually.[9]

10. **Your people's loudest gripe is about job burnout.** A culture that lacks a deliberate focus on maintaining a healthy *work/life balance* is often characterized by low staff morale, high employee

burnout, and lower than average production from the workforce. It is a quality often seen in an organization needing a cultural transformation.

While Amazon continues to dominate, its culture is often the subject of ridicule because of the unrelenting pace and high demands placed on its staff. It has even been reported that Amazon warehouse workers are afraid to go to the bathroom or take a sick day for fear that their nearly unattainable productivity targets will be missed, and they will be fired.[10]

If this kind of workplace imbalance remains an issue, it could become Amazon's Achilles' heel.

To put all of this in perspective, if your company shows two or three of these signs, it probably needs some cultural improvement work right away. If you're afflicted by four or five of these, there's no doubt that you need some objective, outside assistance to remedy the situation. But if you've nodded your head at six or more of these points, your culture requires an overhaul. If you don't take action, forget about becoming indispensable.

The good news is that you don't have to go it alone. There are firms like mine (Indispensable Consulting) that can help. Let me share a six-step approach we developed that is specifically aimed at transforming a company's culture.

Culture Reset™

The premise of the approach that I am about to share with you is simple: top decision-makers have a choice.

They can let their firm's existing culture evolve naturally and take whatever form that it may (as every culture does, if not thoughtfully shape-shifted), or they can design their company's culture in a deliberate and rigorous way and craft the culture that they need to become indispensable.

The Culture Reset™ Methodology delivers a Culture Transformation Plan. The work is done through a series of phases as follows:

1. **Project initiation** formally establishes project roles/responsibilities and commences the project.
2. **Strategic framework setting** develops a set of business principles that state senior leadership's preferences for how it wants to manage the company's cultural evolution.
3. **Baselining** assesses the current company culture and work setting and characterizes its existing people, processes, and technology from a company culture perspective.
4. **Target visioning** defines the target cultural environment.
5. **Gap analysis** determines the gaps between baseline and target cultural settings.
6. **Implementation planning** identifies and prioritizes the work needed to implement the projects and programs identified.
7. **Plan administration design** recommends a process for managing the execution of all of the strategic initiatives identified in the Culture Transformation Plan.
8. **Project completion** formally delivers the final plan to the organization.

Interviews, surveys and workshops are conducted with a good cross-section of staff from senior leaders to middle management to frontline workers. These provide the means for gaining insight and understanding as well as harnessing leadership's and staff's participation and commitment to the culture change effort.

Work Products Produced

There are six major work products produced during a Culture Reset™ initiative. I will share a sample of each from one of my recent engagements. Of course, the client identity has been changed to maintain anonymity. We will simply refer to them as *the company*.

With that, the following six work products are created through the use of Indispensable Consulting's Culture Reset™ approach:

1. *Culture Reset™ Principles*

This refers to a set of leadership principles for use in driving cultural transformation. Think of them as top leadership's guidelines for how they want the culture to look and feel. These are developed by gaining insights from one-on-one interviews with each member of the senior leadership team.

The interviews are then synthesized, and common themes are identified. It is here that the magic begins—a set of pertinent Culture Reset™ Principles are written specifically for the organization.

Here's an example:

Principle

The next generation of staff is the company's most valued and leveraged asset.

Rationale

The company's competitiveness will be a function of the engagement and change-readiness of its high-potential staff. Opportunities to develop and broaden their skills and responsibilities will be expected. Top talent will not choose our company unless they are clear on how to advance, engaged in important company decisions, and confident in their manager's ability to support their innovative potential.

Implications

- Recruiting processes must evolve to expand the pool of talent, target individuals willing to adapt themselves to growth and advancement opportunities, and involve functional leaders and peers alongside HR staff.
- We must be willing to invest in the development of people and talent at every level. This will require active listening by managers so as to adequately identify where training is most needed and desired, while training new managers on change management and other leadership skills.

- Criteria for reward and promotion will need to be clear, universally understood, and based on the results that people deliver in their roles. Managers and staff at every level should know how the people at every other level are evaluated.
- Management must be prepared and empowered to make tough decisions and take actions with nonperformers. Leadership will need to communicate that they will not tolerate poor performers because of their negative impact on high performers and overall company performance.

Notice that the principle statement is supported by a simple rationale (think of this as answering the question "Why do we need this principle?") and a short list of implications (think of these as addressing the question "What must we be willing to do to make this principle a reality?").

The intent is to provide a set of cultural guidelines for behavior that staff can grasp and begin to act on. Behavioral changes reset cultures.

2. *Culture Baseline*

This refers to an assessment and characterization of your existing cultural landscape. This is done through both an automated assessment tool that surveys a cross-section of staff and solicits opinions on the current state of the organizational culture and a series of workshops with managers and supervisors aimed at gaining their perspective on the organization's current work environment.

Here is a short sample of what may be contained in the Culture Baseline work product:

Integrity and Trust Issues

- Some departments have voiced an opinion that top leadership is not hearing them. The sense of teamwork and willingness to compromise appears to be contributing to an "us versus them" mentality.

- Some staff feel that "office politics" prevents work from being done in the most expedient way.
- Some staff are hesitant to speak up about departmental concerns for fear of being labeled as malcontents.

Communication Issues

- Simply put, communication is ineffective throughout the company. It seems there are issues both within and across departments and there is a lack of effort toward resolving them.

Notice the free-form nature of the commentary presented in the excerpt. Short, bulleted paragraphs organized by themes are all that is needed to characterize the current cultural environment in an organization. The typical Culture Baseline deliverable may cover fifteen to twenty themes and document fifty to sixty issues.

3. *Culture Reset™ Story*

This is a compelling and vivid cultural vision and call to action delivered through detailed and explicit storytelling. The Culture Reset™ Story is created by leveraging the Culture Reset™ Principles developed earlier in the effort and the findings brought to light in the Culture Baseline work, which creates fodder for a series of shorter workshops with the senior leadership team. The culture vision story is cultivated through these workshop discussions.

Here's a short excerpt from the Culture Reset™ Story developed with the client:

An "In It Together" Management Style Is in Place

The old ways of running the company have given way to a new style of business management. The new style can be characterized as one where we're "in it together." Leaders and management are there to set direction and enable success. The new style welcomes collaboration and encourages calculated risk-taking, as long as all of the issues are well understood and the actions to be taken are consistent with the way the senior leadership team wants to conduct business. Employees and teams are rewarded for offering innovative solutions in all that they do.

Cultural and Intellectual Diversity Provides New Capital

The company has transformed into a homogenous whole, where cultural differences and diversity of thought are celebrated and there are many opportunities to share ideas to leverage strengths and minimize the barriers to understanding. An appreciation for new ways of thinking and acting have been adopted.

Here again, notice the punchy style presented in the excerpt. Its short, descriptive paragraphs, separated into sections (which serve to highlight key characteristics of the new culture) make for easy consumption. The tone is positive, and it is written as if the company has already reset its culture. A solid Culture Reset™ Story is typically ten to fifteen pages in length and addresses the themes that emerged in the Culture Baseline documentation.

4. *Culture Gap Analysis*

This work compares and contrasts the *current* and the *target* company cultures and identifies gaps between the two that must be filled in order for the firm to achieve its vision. In turn, these gaps are translated into potential project or program initiatives needed to institutionalize the transformative change imagined in the Culture Reset™ Story.

A template, like the one outlined here, is used to capture each idea for closing the identified gaps.

A Project Brief Template is the first step toward documenting a new opportunity for consideration. The completion of the template ensures that opportunities are documented in a consistent format for cross comparison. It includes the following:

- Name—a brief name for the opportunity;
- Description—a description that presents the value of pursuing the opportunity;
- Objectives—covers what the project is intended to accomplish;
- Criticality—defines the importance of the program/project to the achievement of the strategic goals of the company;
- Team/time required—provides first-cut headcount and duration estimates;
- Risks—identifies any potential issues that could result should the program/project be pursued and any risks that may transpire should the initiative not be achieved; and
- Interdependencies—lists other programs/projects that are interrelated with this opportunity.

There are usually about fifteen potential project opportunities identified and documented through this process.

5. *Culture Reset™ Plan*

The potential initiatives identified through the gap analysis are vetted with top leaders, and a road map, which outlines the game plan for cultural transformation, is developed next.

The Culture Reset™ Plan is comprised of individual, detailed project plans for each of the project opportunities that pass muster with the leadership team. The initiatives are then placed on an execution timeline in priority order.

I know that you have all seen detailed project-planning task lists and Gantt charts, so I won't share a sample of these. However, I will share that the company adopted twelve projects of the sixteen project opportunities that were presented. We bundled those twelve into three groups. The projects within each group were then organized across an eighteen-month time horizon. To net it out, the Culture Reset™ Plan for the company included twelve projects to be staffed, funded, and executed over the next four and a half years.

6. *Culture Reset™ Plan Governance Framework*

A company's culture evolves over time as each initiative is accomplished.

Because things change, a structure for monitoring and adjusting your Culture Reset™ Plan to ensure uninterrupted strategic alignment is needed. This is accomplished by putting a Plan Governance Framework in place. It is here that the responsibility for maintaining the Culture Reset™ Plan is designated and processes for review and modification to the Culture Reset™ Plan are put into place.

In this case, the company already had an operational project management office (PMO), so we simply used the PMO to administer the plan. Had this not been the case, we would have recommended the following:

1. Establish a PMO.
2. Designate a leader to manage the unit.
3. Place the unit under a member of the senior leadership team.
4. Develop and institutionalize the processes needed to
   - staff and review ongoing project execution
   - introduce new culture initiatives to the plan
   - adjust priorities
   - include senior leadership sponsorship and review throughout

This is the kind of governance needed to ensure that the Culture Reset™ Plan delivers the results needed to transform the company's culture.

By the way, while my client enters its second year of its Culture Reset™ Plan, I am proud to share that the first two projects have been a fine success and that they have added an additional three new projects as a result. It is great to see how they have worked their plan and continue to fine-tune it over time.

How to Fine-Tune the Culture to Gain Indispensability

Once the plan is created and the proper governance elements are in place, you can work to fine-tune the Culture Reset™ Plan as your culture is implemented. Inevitably, things in your world will change, and you'll need to adjust the plan to accommodate these changes.

Here are eight important cultural levers that every management team has at its disposal to set cultural direction and manage the changes that are necessary to *reset* the company culture:

1. **Strategic alignment** is used to ensure that management and staff are engaged and understand the strategic direction of the organization.

   This lever includes:
   - communicating a vision that motivates the staff,
   - promoting an "outside-in" point of view that emphasizes how a firm is viewed through the lens of the customer,
   - mapping work activities against the achievement of the organization's strategic vision;
   - aligning measurements and rewards with the strategies of the organization and emphasizing results over effort, and
   - recognizing and celebrating strategic achievements as they occur.

   Consider Zappos—the e-tailer goes out of its way to ensure that everyone working there understands that customer service is the key strategic driver and customer delight is the ultimate measurement of success. Its culture is clearly aligned with its customer-centric strategic drivers.

2. **Leadership tendencies** covers how leaders choose to lead.

   This lever consists of:
   - leaders demonstrating their commitment to the people of the organization,
   - establishing team-based operating models to support problem-solving and getting the job done,
   - adopting a virtual "no spin zone" within the company to minimize internal politics and curb the promotion of parochial points of view,
   - actively communicating and engaging with staff to enable a fuller understanding of the organization's goals and priorities, and
   - stamping out bad behaviors by management and staff.

Gary Whited, recently retired president, and his former COO and current president, Danny Deep, have done an outstanding job at GDLS in actively communicating and engaging with staff at the defense company. Besides their annual leadership retreat, which gathers more than fifty of their top managers to discuss vision and strategy, the pair often attend departmental project meetings to show support and offer guidance. Hands-on leaders like Whited and Deep create the *esprit de corps* needed to build an indispensable business.

3. **Focus orientation** relates to where leaders place emphasis.

    This lever contains:

    - establishing a strong sense of "being in it together" within the organization;
    - the building of a "Do your job" mind-set, which encourages staff to develop a sense of being duty-bound to do their jobs at the highest level possible for the sake of their coworkers;
    - promoting collaboration among management and staff;
    - placing a high value on transparency, both internally and externally; and
    - demonstrating that excellence is a top priority.

    Regardless of what you may think of him or his team, New England Patriots' head coach Bill Belichick's "Do your job!" philosophy—characterized by being prepared, working hard, paying attention to the details, and putting the team first—is worth learning more about because of what it can offer to leaders who are trying to establish a winning culture.

    Belichick is the only head coach to win six Super Bowl titles. His career winning percentage of .691 is the highest in NFL history. He is certainly doing something right in shaping the culture at the Patriots!

4. **Risk appetite** explores how deviations from the status quo are tolerated by the organization.

    This lever encompasses:

    - encouraging staff to take action and make decisions without seeking management's preapproval,

- allowing staff to "test" new ways of thinking and doing without fear of reprisal,
- providing ample opportunity for employees to freely advance in their jobs and careers,
- establishing mechanisms for newly hired and younger staff to have a voice in how work can be improved and performed, and
- enabling the organization to learn through its experiences so that past mistakes are rarely repeated.

For instance, Google's culture of innovation can be characterized by its willingness, as Frederik Pferdt, its chief innovation evangelist puts it, "to establish an environment where people can share ideas which might not be finished, might not be perfect, but are attempts to start disrupting things, to start a discussion of things that may be impossible at the moment."[11]

It is the kind of cultural imperative needed to delight. It is also indicative of a culture that is not risk-averse and, consequently, delivers breakthrough innovations to the marketplace.

5. **Innovation leverage** is concerned with knowing how emerging ideas and technologies are used within the organization.

This lever covers:

- investing in ideas that will differentiate the organization in the marketplace,
- providing staff with the tools needed to do their jobs at their highest potential,
- regularly changing and adjusting work processes to improve performance,
- constantly monitoring the work environment to identify opportunities to automate and digitize work activities, and
- becoming data-driven and leveraging information to help make decisions, forging new ideas and defining new directions within the organization.

USAA, the financial services business out of San Antonio, Texas, is a company that encourages innovative thinking. Case in point, a security guard working at USAA authored, during his tenure, *twenty-five* fully realized patents for his company.[12] It's no wonder that the firm, known for its great working environment, has appeared on *Fortune*'s World's Most Admired Companies list for the past six years in a row.

Innovation leverage is a key cultural factor in becoming indispensable. In USAA's case, even the guy at the door feels empowered to develop and contribute his thinking to the betterment of the company.

6. **Change adaptability** examines how change is introduced and managed within an organization.

This lever entails:

- broadly communicating all significant change efforts within the organization to remove all wonder and doubt about the effort;
- managing work as a series of projects and programs that enable the organization to move toward the achievement of its vision;
- aggressively leveraging the free-agent marketplace by hiring experts, consultants. and provisional staff on a temporary basis to enable business success;
- deepening and streamlining the interrelationships among strategic partners, vendors, distributors, and customers; and
- encouraging staff resiliency in the face of constant change.

Waffle House, Inc. is headquartered in Norcross, Georgia. The restaurant chain has 2,100 locations in twenty-five states. Most of the locations are in the South, where the chain is considered a cultural icon. It is also a terrific example of a company that has built a resilient culture that uses communication to keep staff in the loop and leverages its network of strategic partners to keep the business up and running, even in the face of natural disasters.

Because the company's reputation to weather the storm is so strong, state, local, and federal governments unofficially use what is called the "Waffle House Index" to gauge storm severity.[13] If the restaurant is open, things look bright. if they're serving a limited menu, there is still work to do. If the restaurant is closed, they've got trouble.

The Waffle House is a company that has built a culture that can handle change, even the kind that it can't control.

7. **Digital capabilities** looks at the use of advanced information technology like data analytics, artificial intelligence, and robotics and characterizes the impact of its use in the workplace.

This lever has the power to redefine how work gets done. Greater use indicates a willingness to seek innovative solutions to business problems. A lack of use may point to a culture that lacks imagination.

Challenged by business impacts brought about by the pandemic, Smart Health Clubs moved its business online, pivoting to provide online engagement solutions to retain members through the pandemic.[14] This move exemplifies a company culture that is open to leveraging digital capabilities as a means of reshaping its operations.

It serves as an interesting example of how digital technology can be used to shift the work culture.

8. **Social impact** examines the degree to which the culture recognizes the importance and promotion of social responsibility.

From taking steps to improve climate change to promoting volunteerism, this cultural lever enhances both the workforce experience and the company's standing in the communities in which it operates.

With more than 2,200 employees, the Warsteiner Group continues to be committed to the German brew art. It is also a firm that takes its social responsibility seriously. It provides funding for cultural events, youth and senior citizen initiatives, charitable work, and sports projects in the town of Warstein, Germany, where it is headquartered.

The Warsteiner Partner Funds is a nonprofit organization that supports projects focusing on children and development aid. Its promotional strategy includes the support of preeminent events in hot air ballooning, equestrian sports, soccer, and handball—all intended to contribute to the betterment of society.

Besides being one of my favorite beers, Warsteiner is an example of a company that puts its money where its mouth is when it comes to supporting its local community.

As mentioned, it is a leader's job to reshape the organizational culture. These eight levers enable you to do that in an effective and transformative way. As you begin to adjust these levers, you'll see breakthroughs begin to occur in your work setting. You will see an organization capable of delivering levels of achievement higher than anyone ever thought possible.

When this occurs, new ways to become indispensable begin to reveal themselves. But watch out for the impediments to change.

There Will Be Impediments to Change

Before we close out our culture discussion, it would be irresponsible of me not to mention the *potholes* that can break an axle while on your journey of reimagining your company culture. Let me share a few of the more common impediments to change that you may encounter.

Here are three of the most common challenges to effective cultural change as seen among recent clients:

1. **Change fatigue:** A topic these days, change fatigue is a very real phenomenon experienced by organizations that have been unable to deliver results from past change initiatives. Consequently, this failure has led to confusion and emotional overload among staff. Thus any cultural change effort falters because of institutional burnout.

   Consider the toll that the coronavirus has had on businesses around the globe. From new mask requirements to temperature monitoring, the pandemic brought about great changes to the workplace. Couple that with the constant *push* from top leadership to deliver in spite of these new stresses and there's little wonder why fatigue has set in among the workforce. A culture shift effort would certainly fail to gain lift without a solid methodology, like the one described earlier, to guide the effort.

Fight change fatigue by using a simple-to-understand and engaging change approach.

2. **Little to no staff engagement:** Many organizations choose to drive cultural change through top-down *telling*. This doesn't work. Simply put, there is a huge difference between communication and engagement. To transform a corporate culture, you must engage everyone in the organization by including them in the process and securing their commitment to change.

   This was definitely an issue with a recent client. Because of the change fatigue, staff members were not engaged at the time the Culture Reset™ initiative was first announced. However, by virtue of the inclusive nature of the approach, we were able to spur on broad swathes of participation among staffers across the company. The effort gathered momentum as project participants began to see their ideas being used by the project team.

   Gain staff engagement by including broad cross-sections of the *rank and file*.

3. **"Flavor of the month" mentality:** There's little doubt that most seasoned professionals have lived through failed change efforts of one form or another during their careers. The thought of participating in another one does little to excite or motivate. So many choose to just "wait it out"—expecting leadership to shift their focus to another "flavor of the month" somewhere down the line.

   This was part of the challenge that we confronted with the client mentioned earlier. The staff had worked with many of the top consulting firms before we were brought in to assist. Nevertheless, our approach proved to be different from the others in one very important way: we did the work of the project *with* them, instead of *for* them.

   Consequently, the team of their people assigned to the effort essentially "owned" the results of the project. In fact, they are well on their way to implementing many of the cultural changes that we identified and put into the plan.

Overcome the "flavor of the month" by cocreating work products with employees.

These are just some of the ways to avoid the impediments to change that you may confront when driving cultural transformation. Now that you better understand what can be expected, I hope that you can avoid any pothole that you may encounter.

Simply be on the lookout for the following:

- **Destabilized execution:** The work needed to drive cultural transformation is time-consuming and intense. In the short term, in fact, the effort can interrupt the work setting as key players are asked to participate. In the long run, though, poor choices when making needed changes (or misfires in how those changes are implemented) can serve to severely disrupt the way work is done well into the future. Therefore, you want your high-performing team to be contributing to the Culture Reset™ effort.
- **Squandered resources:** Similarly, the time, people, and money spent on ill-conceived or poorly executed cultural transformation initiatives are resources that you can't get back—that waste can be tallied in both the true costs of time and money as well as missed opportunities (where those squandered resources could have been put to better use). Be sure you know how you're going to drive the project before you kick it off.
- **Lowered morale:** If the result of the initiative bears no fruit, employee morale will, most certainly, take a hit—lots of buildup and no follow-through will be the prevailing opinion among the rank and file.

Just remember what to do to avoid these potholes:

1. Use a proven, **structured methodology,** like Culture Reset™, to remove any guesswork from the equation.

2. Don't leave your culture to chance. Instead, **deliberately culti-vate** your corporate culture to position your organization for bold success.

3. Seek out **expert advice** from people who do this kind of company culture overhaul for a living. Experts in the field can help you avoid the major ruts in the road because their experience helps them anticipate where the nastiest ones are before you do.

To Close

Company culture is influenced by the preferences and leadership style of the senior management team. These preferences and styles are passed down from generation to generation of worker through myth and legend—much like a country's culture emerges through the stories that its people tell each other. To change the narrative of your company, culture must be transformed deliberately and be reset to be indispensable.

Once you get the culture *right*, the focus needs to shift to the *people* who comprise the enterprise. We will cover that agenda item in the next chapter.

Chapter 4's Indispensable Top Ten List

This chapter is loaded with great content and insight. This is a list of the top ten takeaways teed up for easy reference. Be sure to take a deeper dive into other key concepts by reviewing the chapter in detail.

1. If you want to be indispensable, you need the right culture. Period. End of sentence.

2. The ROI of culture change can only be calculated by determining the value of a stronger, more vibrant business—one that is strategically aligned, team-based, transparent, resilient, and customer-centric. It is the sum of those parts that define the return on your cultural investment.

3. Company culture must be fashioned in a very deliberate way to avoid all kinds of problematic consequences, including poor performance, weak company affiliation, and worker burnout, to name a few.

4. Top decision-makers don't have to drive cultural change alone. There are experts available who can help manage the change. Just be sure that the experts hired to help bring with them a sound approach to guide the culture-planning effort.

5. A solid culture plan is comprised of individual, detailed project plans aimed at shape-shifting key aspects of your culture. The initiatives are then placed on an execution timeline.

6. A Plan Governance Framework must be put in place upon completion of the Culture Reset™ Plan. This framework lays out the responsibilities and processes needed to keep the plan aligned with the evolving strategic intentions of the leadership team.

7. Inevitably, things in the world change, and you'll need to fine-tune the plan to accommodate these changes. There are eight levers available to leaders for incrementally adjusting the culture plan over time, including focus orientation, risk appetite, and digital capabilities.

8. There will be impediments to change. They manifest themselves in the form of change fatigue, low staff engagement, and a "flavor of the month" mentality.

9. These potholes can be avoided by selecting an easy-to-understand approach that engages a broad swath of staffers and is characterized by a commitment to cocreate work products with the people who will ultimately be responsible for executing the changes identified in the culture transformation plan.

10. To change the narrative of your company, culture must be transformed deliberately and be reset to be indispensable.

CHAPTER 5

The Right People

ATTRACTING AND RETAINING THE "RIGHT" people is next on the agenda.

Now that you think that you've created a great company culture, I bet you think your work here is done. Well, I'm here to tell you that your work has only just begun.

You have to deal with those pesky people. You know the ones—they work for you!

Hey, I get it. We all want to believe that we are exceptional leaders and that our people are eager to do their best every day. But sometimes we can't see the reality of the situation. Our personal blind spots get in the way. In fact, sometimes we're not all that engaging and our people aren't as satisfied with their jobs as we like to think.

Don't believe me? Let's put the theory to a test. Let's survey your people. Here are five straightforward yes or no questions:

1. Are you happy to work here?
2. Are you inspired to do your best for the company?
3. Do you ever think about working anywhere else?
4. Do you think this company is the best place for you to work?
5. Would you recommend the company to a friend who's looking for a job?

Scoring the results from this type of casual staff survey will speak volumes—lots of agreement, and all is fine, continue doing what you're doing; lots of divergence, you've got a problem, and it's time for some changes. If you don't change things and get the "right" people and unequivocally engage them, there's no way you're ever going to become indispensable.

I'm going to go out on a limb and assume that you're like most leaders and your staff is not as engaged as you may like to think. In fact, according to a recent Gallup study, "53% of workers are in the 'not engaged' category. They may be generally satisfied but are not cognitively and emotionally connected to their work and workplace; they will usually show up to work and do the minimum required but will quickly leave their company for a slightly better offer."[1]

That said, let me proceed with some thoughts on how to get the "right" people and captivate them in such a way as to get the best out of everyone.

Where to Begin?

I bet you know your company's value proposition. You probably have it down to a one-liner that you can rattle off at a moment's notice. Your *employee value proposition* is another story altogether. You probably don't have that on the tip of your tongue unless you work in the HR department, and even then, it may be difficult to spout off.

I'm here to suggest that perhaps this should change.

In the end, your employee value proposition (EVP) is of vital importance in attracting and retaining the kind of talent that you need to be indispensable!

Defining Your EVP

EVP is the value that staffers gain in return for their work—and it's not all about compensation. Consider it in terms of Maslow's hierarchy of needs.

Abraham Maslow proffered in his paper "A Theory of Human Motivation," published in *Psychological Review*[2] back in 1943, that a person was motivated through the satisfaction of a set of needs that ranged from the elementary to the truly urbane. For example, *food* and *shelter* needs have to be met before *belonging* and *esteem* needs would ever motivate a person, and those needs have to be satisfied prior to one's pursuit of *self-actualization*, the idea of living to one's maximum potential.

EVP should be considered in similar terms, as follows:

- **Compensation/benefits:** Your compensation model is the lowest rung in the hierarchy. It addresses meeting your people's basic needs. Think of salary, incentives, and wealth-sharing being the *food*, while health, retirement, and personal-leave policies are the *shelter* in Maslow's hierarchy.

  Capital One, headquartered in McLean, Virginia, is one of the most popular online banks in the country, and according to comparably.com, its staff feels properly compensated. Capital One made Comparably's top ten list of highest-rated companies for best compensation in 2019 (based on employee feedback gathered on a variety of questions regarding the topic). The median compensation there is $149,882, and its HR and marketing departments are among the most satisfied staff members in the bank.[3]

  Proper compensation and benefits are part of the indispensability equation.

- **Career path / recognition programs:** This part of your EVP strategy plays a compulsory role in staff retention. Staff feel a stronger connection to your work community through the provision of the "right" kinds of job titles, training, career paths, and employee appreciation efforts. Their need for *belonging* is met if these policies are well-designed and implemented.

  The Business Development Bank of Canada (BDC) is Canada's only bank devoted exclusively to entrepreneurs. BDC wanted to ensure that their 2,300 staffers' experience was enriching and engaging. So the bank launched a recognition strategy that included a new online platform that featured a custom yearbook, allowing leaders and peers to add comments to an employee's personalized booklet throughout the year. The result is greater recognition of an individual and the results that they produce.[4]

Satisfying staff's *belonging* needs is an important ingredient in creating an indispensable business.

- **Work elements:** The "right" kind of workplace environment, highlighted by a variety of assignments, autonomy, and the occasion to provide input, enables an employee's *esteem* needs to be satisfied. Staffers feel better about themselves when they are given new and varied opportunities to contribute.

  For example, Screwfix, the largest multichannel retailer of trade tools, accessories, and hardware products in the UK, enables its employees to provide feedback to their managers on a biweekly basis. There are no rules or guidelines on how or what feedback to provide. Instead, staff give feedback on everything, including how things are going, how they think things are being managed, how the company interacts with customers, and ideas for improvement.[5] Many ideas provided have been implemented through these feedback sessions.

  Your staff's *esteem* needs must be addressed in order to become indispensable.

- **Pride in affiliation:** By ensuring that your organization is something your personnel can be proud to be part of goes a long way in satisfying their need for *self-actualization*. EVP considerations include such things as company values, brand reputation, and community involvement.

  The U.S. Marine Corps (USMC), for instance, is the epitome of an organization that builds pride in affiliation. From its iconic slogan, "The few, the proud," to its mission of defending the country, the USMC has what it takes to prompt its people to voluntarily put their lives on the line for the sake of the job.

Now, I'm not saying you should build a company that mirrors the USMC. However, I am suggesting that you strive to establish the feeling of pride, fellowship, and common loyalty that the Marine Corps builds in its marines.

Address these elements of meeting your people's hierarchy of needs and you'll be well on your way to attracting and retaining the best talent available on the planet—just be sure to notice that building a juice bar is nowhere on the list!

Really? A Juice Bar Is Not the Answer?

Sure, you can invest in building a dog-friendly skate park right in the middle of the foyer in your company headquarters and encourage your staff to take a snooze in those fancy nap pods that you bought on Amazon, but none of these so-called engagement devices is the answer to getting and keeping the right people.

No doubt, there are many modern ideas about what companies need to do to attract talent and engage workers. Up until last year, it was quite fashionable for your facilities to sport all kinds of stimulating features like in-house juice bars and outdoor jungle gyms, though those are steadily falling out of favor due to COVID-19. Of course, there are other, more modest options to drive staff engagement.

Here are a few:

1. **Craft, distribute, and tell your vision story:** As described in earlier chapters, employee engagement begins with a compelling story to which people can relate. Develop one and tell it using all of the means possible to heighten staff engagement. Your goal should be to provide everyone in your organization with the opportunity to receive and understand your story.

    In fact, according to Jim Clifton, chairman and CEO of Gallup, "The new, younger workforce wants their work to have deep mission and purpose—and they don't want old-style command-and-control bosses. They want coaches who inspire them, communicate with them frequently, and develop their strengths."[6]

If you want to become indispensable, you better have a vision that includes this kind of leadership dynamic, and you must communicate that vision so your people understand the potential.

2. **Place focus on the outside:** Whether real or imagined, a sense that an "enemy" wants to destroy the company will inspire your people to work together to defeat that adversary. In turn, this will engage your team in the work at hand.

   Apple is the poster child for this kind of thinking. Upon his return to Apple, Steve Jobs saved the company he had been ousted from by creating an *underdog* mentality within the firm. As a result, Apple fundamentally changed the computing, music, and smartphone industries forever.

3. **Promote "give and take":** Ditch the command-and-control behavior as soon as you can. People know who the boss is; you don't need to remind them upon every interaction. Instead, promote open and honest two-way communication and your people will gain trust in you and become more engaged with their work.

   Skillshare CEO Michael Karnjanaprakorn wrote about this topic in a recent article:

> In the early days at Skillshare, we were at a crossroads with a very big decision. Should we keep the business offline or should we move the business online? We had a whole offsite [meeting] dedicated to this decision and not surprisingly, the team was split right down the middle.
>
> We encouraged everyone to express their opinions and challenge all of our assumptions. There was a lot of tension throughout the process, but the end result of that tension created an open, transparent, and trusting team.

Without going through the rigorous debate, we might not have made that decision to go online as deliberately. This deep level of debate only works when everyone leaves their egos outside of the room. That's why humility is so important to our culture.

Decision-making isn't about getting feedback from everyone to reach 100% consensus. It's about giving everyone a chance to participate. We might not all agree with the final decision, but we should feel like our perspectives were considered.[7]

Skillshare's decision-making approach appears to be working out quite well. Its online learning community boasts more than four million students and offers more than twenty thousand classes.

4. **Enable success:** Do all that you can to knock out the roadblocks that are impeding your team's success. Once people see that you're dedicated to making them successful, they'll become more committed to getting the job done for you.

Nordstrom is a company that practices this leadership approach. The notion that leaders are there to enable team success is baked into its college intern orientation. These future leaders learn about the importance of Nordstrom's inverted pyramid (which places floor staff at the highest level of importance and the executive team and directors at the lowest level) and servant leadership.[8]

The goal is to encourage its potential future store managers to adopt the values that have made Nordstrom a preferred department store among discerning customers for many years. As a loyal customer, I think it's working.

5. **Ask:** People like it when you show them enough respect to ask them for their opinion. So ask your team what else can be done to improve the company culture and make the work setting more compelling and satisfying. Having this type of ongoing dialogue not only helps gain staff commitment; it also harvests some good ideas for advancing the business environment.

Virgin is a company known for asking questions and listening to its employees. It's a winning approach—the organization keeps learning, and employees feel important and are engaged.

According to its chairman, Richard Branson, "A company is people . . . employees want to know . . . am I being listened to or am I a cog in the wheel? People really need to feel wanted."[9]

This mentality is one of the reasons that Virgin continues to be one of the most respected businesses on the planet.

6. **Celebrate achievement:** Don't forget to celebrate and recognize all of the small successes that come along the way during the year. Make sure to let your staffers know and appreciate all that they do to help your business become indispensable. Public recognition, whether it be ceremonial, placed in company newsletters, or posted on websites, goes a long way in showing that you care.

   At Zappos, staff are given the authority, for example, to award bonuses to one another without any management review or sign-off. When an employee sees a coworker going *above and beyond*, they have can reward that employee with an extra $50. It's a great way to celebrate achievement at the grassroots level, and it drives employee commitment.

7. **Empower decision-making:** Trust and enthusiasm build when well-trained frontline personnel are put in a position to make decisions that stick. It shows that you have their back, and that motivates people to go the extra mile for the business.

   At Costco, employees have the power to take back returned items, make exchanges, and ensure purchasing issues get resolved at the point of sale—even without a receipt. This makes Costco's frontline staff feel empowered and part of a team that doesn't need to get permission from a higher-up to get their job done.

With that, I hope that these more fundamental engagement ideas work for you. After thirty-plus years of consulting, I am confident that they will—whether you install a climbing wall in your office or not!

Of course, who you hire matters just as much as your engagement approach. Let's look at that next.

Big hint: when in doubt, hire the ambitious.

Hiring the Ambitious

Do you believe that most people are rightly satisfied working just hard enough to gain a desired quality of life? I believe it. In fact, I don't think ambition can be taught. Either you have it or you don't.

Further, I think most people are not naturally ambitious. Like most of the human condition, ambition likely follows a bell curve. As I see it, there is a small minority of *highly enterprising people* on one end of the curve and another small minority of *slackers* on the other end, with most everybody else sitting somewhere in the middle.

It's quite a quandary for business leaders wanting to cultivate an indispensable organization.

What do you do? Hire for ambition.

Why? When the chips are down, you want people who are hungry for achievement. Those kinds of people don't accept losing easily, and they are committed to success.

How can you find the naturally ambitious? Here are five questions that you can ask an applicant at your next interview. Their answers will indicate where they may fall on the ambition curve:[10]

1. **Do you think you're going to win when you play a game with your friends?** Most ambitious people would answer yes to this question. They believe that they have what it takes to win in nearly every setting.

2. **Do you know what you want to achieve professionally?** People with immense professional desire know what they want and are constantly striving to get it. If a candidate can't articulate what they want from themselves, they may not have what you need for your business. You're looking for people who possess a very specific, unalterable goal.

3. **Would you sacrifice social acceptance among your peers to achieve an important personal objective?** The most ambitious people are willing to sacrifice anything to achieve their goals. This question *tests* the candidate on their readiness to pay the price in the short term for the promise of gains in the future. If you find people who are willing to put in the work in order to win, your organization will wind up winning most of the time.

4. **Would you be happier in a job with less pay and responsibility, or one with more pay and immense responsibility?** This question gets at the candidate's desire for achievement. If they seek less responsibility, they may be a "middle of the curve" person who is seeking the comfort zone, and they may not be the enterprising person you're looking for to round out your team of high performers. On the other hand, if they tell you that they want to take full responsibility for winning, you know you have a person who has true desire.

5. **Have you ever felt content with your life?** Ambitious people are always looking for the next hill to climb. Feeling content is fleeting at best for those with the greatest desire for achievement. It is with this kind of question that we can see a person's *true grit* and ambition come out.

I hope that you use these questions to help you make better hiring decisions—finding people who are adequately motivated to help you achieve business indispensability.

Of course, being blindly ambitious with no emotional control doesn't make an ideal teammate either. Indeed, you want to find well-rounded people who possess the necessary emotional maturity to attract followers and lead others. For this reason, put emotional intelligence high in your personnel search criteria too.

Emotional Intelligence Quotient

People with high emotional intelligence quotients (EQ) are great listeners and are easy to talk with. In fact, they tend to be strong communicators in both the written and spoken word. People with high EQs are ones who just seem comfortable with who they are. They are masters in conflict resolution and can de-escalate situations before they get out of hand. These people regulate their reactions, keeping their cool no matter what comes up. High EQ contributors are priceless to a business because they are habitually modest and unassuming. Indeed, these are the people you need to become indispensable.

In fact, TalentSmart, an EQ assessment firm, tested more than one million people and found that 90 percent of high performers had high EQs and earned on average $29,000 more per year.[11] I'd suggest that there's something to building a team around high-EQ people.

Here are some of the key ways high-EQ individuals can make a difference in making your business indispensable:

1. **Their consideration for others improves communications:** Empathetic people tend to have a knack for connecting with others and can quickly establish an open and honest dialogue. This skill is invaluable in any work setting.

   After assertions of a higher-than-average injury rate at Tesla's Fremont factory, for example, CEO Elon Musk urged workers to report all injuries, adding that he would personally visit the factory floor and perform the same tasks as injured Tesla staff.

   Take a look at the email he sent to workers:

   > No words can express how much I care about your safety and wellbeing. It breaks my heart when someone is injured building cars and trying their best to make Tesla successful.
   >
   > Going forward, I've asked that every injury be reported directly to me, without exception. I'm meeting with the safety team every week and would like to meet every injured person as soon as they are well so that I can understand from them exactly what we need to do to make it better. I will then go down to the production line and perform the same task that they perform.

This is what all managers at Tesla should do as a matter of course. At Tesla, we lead from the front line, not from some safe and comfortable ivory tower. Managers must always put their team's safety above their own.[12]

Powerful stuff, communicated with empathy and a willingness to make things right—it served to ease the tension among concerned staff.

2. **They're great under pressure:** When things go south, you can count on a high-EQ person to get the job done. They have a certain *grace under pressure* that far too few people can ever hope to emulate.

New Zealand prime minister Jacinda Ardern provides a wonderful example of a high-EQ leader in action.

On March 15, 2019, more than fifty people were massacred at two mosques in Christchurch, New Zealand, by a suspected white supremacist. Arden called for swift changes to the nation's gun laws. It was a bold political move in a country where acquiring a semiautomatic weapon is relatively easy. Less than a month later, New Zealand's parliament voted 119 to 1 to change the country's gun laws.

Not every leader can maintain such poise and be so effective under pressure. But it's a characteristic that can make your company indispensable.

3. **They generate trust in the workplace and marketspace through diplomacy:** Tact is priceless in any work setting. Trust is built with a delicate touch. Thoughtfulness and discretion are rewarded in kind. High EQ people build high trust among everyone they work with.

When Starbucks chose to close more than eight thousand stores for a day in 2018 for racial bias training weeks after two black men were arrested at a Philadelphia Starbucks for loitering, many rolled their eyes and wrote it off as a crisis management stunt. The move cost the company millions. However, the fact that Starbucks CEO

Kevin Johnson put his money where his mouth was demonstrated the type of tactful diplomacy that generates trust. The company ranked fifth on *Fortune* magazine's World's Most Admired Companies list the following year.

4. **They like to co-create:** High EQ staffers seek out opportunities to collaborate. Their innate willingness to co-create the best solutions to nagging problems with teammates makes them *favorites* among colleagues and customers alike.

5. **Their charismatic personality improves team performance:** High EQ people tend to lead by example. This trait inspires others to deliver results too. For this reason, high-performance teams tend to be stacked with high-EQ talent.

   England's National Health System (NHS) delivers health-care services through a network of Clinical Commissioning Groups (CCGs). Each CCG is responsible for overseeing service delivery to patients within various geographical locations. The North London CCG is headed up by Helen Pettersen. At the height of the pandemic last year, her charismatic leadership impact was described this way by one of her college interns: "Charisma is important now more than ever. For me, charisma embodies several concepts including excellent communication skills, confidence, accountability, and strong convictions. Leadership that I have borne witness to during the pandemic has shown me that charisma, at a time where people are often lacking motivation, plays a fundamental role in inspiring me."[13]

   If a college student can pick up on the importance of charisma, we should be able to appreciate its value too.

6. **They are *natural-born leaders*:** High EQ talent possesses leadership capabilities, which improves outcomes. Their ability to influence others is instrumental in them gaining followership. Developing and promoting high-EQ people enables a business to establish the kind of leadership foundation needed to drive indispensable behaviors across the business.

To reiterate, fielding an emotionally intelligent team is a key means to winning in the marketplace. Clearly, companies need these kinds of people to lead others to victory. Indeed, they need these kinds of people to set the example and further instill the "right" values and work ethic.

"Customer First" Is the Most Important Value

The best, most indispensable companies impart all kinds of important values to their workforce. Keeping promises, being fair, and encouraging teamwork are usually among the top philosophies being promoted these days. However, there is no value more essential to becoming indispensable in the marketplace than putting the customer first.

It makes sense, right? Your people are the ones who delight your customer. Indeed, it is staffers who make customers want to do business with you.

When a problem call is received, that staff member *becomes* the company in the mind of that customer. If the customer has an exceptional experience, the customer loves the company. If not, they just may take their business elsewhere in the near future.

For this reason, you want to become the company that attracts and retains extraordinary talent. We've already covered several important aspects of how to do this; here are a few more ideas that can help you reinforce the "customer first" attitude among your team.

Flip the pyramid! Like the example shared about Nordstrom earlier in the chapter, your view of what's important to your business needs to include customers at the top of the pyramid. The people who work directly with the customer comprise the next rung. Those who work in support of those who work with customers follow next—by the way, you're at the bottom because your role is to serve everyone else!

Redefine what "good" service looks like. Any business can adopt traditional customer satisfaction practices—those things that make for timely, accurate, and objective service delivery. What you need is to redefine what "excellent service" means.

Here's a great example of how one store manager at Trader Joe's in Wayne, Pennsylvania, went above and beyond to help a customer in his time of need.[14]

An eighty-nine-year-old man was stuck in his house during a snowstorm, and his granddaughter was worried he wouldn't have enough food. She called around to several grocery stores and asked if they would deliver, to no avail. Finally, Trader Joe's said they normally don't deliver, but they would help. She read off a big list to the store manager, and they delivered the entire order and more within thirty minutes, free of charge.[15]

That's customer service. That's how you become indispensable. Just ask the eighty-nine-year-old man and his granddaughter.

Heighten the concept of servicing internal customers too! By placing emphasis on the internal customer throughout your company's value chain, you enhance the ability to deliver superior service to the external ones who pay the bills. When everyone on your team operates at first-rate levels, employee satisfaction and customer quality go through the roof.

Spread the wealth. Creative recognitions and rewards enhance employee performance. These are necessary ingredients for motivating frontline personnel. They assist in achieving peak performance. After all, people want to be recognized and rewarded for exceptional work. Reinvest in your people through solid bonus and compensation programs.

CA Technologies, a $4.5 billion business software and solutions company, has adopted a program that rewards different types of behavior over time. Early on, employees might be rewarded for participating in customer service training. Next, they might be rewarded for closing the loop with unhappy customers. Later, they might be rewarded for the number of customer problems they resolve.[16]

By adopting a program like this one, companies share the wealth as their workforces become more adept at delivering the kind of service that makes for indispensability in the marketplace.

Promote an ongoing commitment through your leadership team's actions. Top leaders are the ambassadors of change. They must consistently support frontline staff, doing whatever they can to pave the way for them to enchant the customer base. This is achieved through action. You can't just talk about putting the customer first—you have to live it. Do that, and you're setting an example for your team to follow.

Continually strengthen the structural underpinnings of your business. Strategies for service delivery require deep-rooted and strong foundations. The company must continue to evolve and forge a work environment where *exceptional service* sets the bar to clear every day.

Take Southwest Airlines, as an example. Part of the way it delivers on its customer service promise is by rethinking its operations. According to a *Harvard Business Review* article on the subject, "Schedules, routes, and company practices (at Southwest Airlines)—such as open seating and the use of simple, color-coded, reusable boarding passes—enable the boarding of three and four times more passengers per day than competing airlines."[17]

Indeed, service delivery is the "table stakes" required to becoming indispensable. And it's your people who will determine if your customers keep coming back or seek a better experience elsewhere. Do what you have to do to help your people *exceed* your customer's expectations.

Where Does the Next-Gen Workforce Fit?

You may not be aware that the Next-Gen workforce is comprised of Gen Y and Gen Z people. Gen Y workers were born between 1980 and 1995. Gen Z workers were born between 1995 and 2010. This makes them the youngest demographic among your current workforce. Because they'll be the people leading your firm next, you need them onboard and committed to ensure lasting indispensability.

However, the Next-Gen worker is known to be willing to leave for *greener pastures* whenever a better opportunity comes along. Their "flight risk" potential puts employers in a bit of a catch-22 situation when it comes to preparing these individuals to be valued contributors. *Why train someone who is going to leave?*

Here are five ideas that you can put to use today to foster the long-term commitment of the Next-Gen workforce.

Institute a Next-Gen committee. Form a committee of younger staff and charge them to plan and host events that feature senior leaders discussing important business issues. This activity helps establish a two-way conversation between Next-Gen staff and their top management, helping the younger staff feel more connected with what's going on at the top of the organization chart. Additionally, the practice provides an opportunity for top leaders to garner ideas and perspective from their younger staffers—enhancing morale and improving retention.

Build a buddy program. This idea centers around pairing Next-Gen staffers with peer "buddies" in the hopes of better assimilating younger staff into the business. Serving as mentors, *buddies* help Next-Gen colleagues learn the ropes and understand the company culture. It should become an essential element of any employee onboarding.

Microsoft recently piloted a buddy program as part of its onboarding strategy and found that it helped new hires in three important ways:[18]

1. Better context for understanding their role and job responsibilities
2. Improved productivity
3. Enhanced employee satisfaction

As a result, the software giant has decided to expand its program by creating an internal site for hiring managers to match new hires with an onboarding buddy.

Host lunch 'n' learn sessions. Like the Next-Gen committee, these can enhance a sense of connection among Next-Gen staff too. Depending on the topic, sessions are cohosted by both younger and more experienced staff. The focus is on providing a short, one-hour overview of a "hot topic" emerging within the business. The practice promotes learning and creates a way to engage younger workers.

Provide tuition debt relief. Offer to pay down college debt of the Next-Gen workforce in exchange for their commitment to remain in the company for a period of time. The longer they stay and produce, the more college debt gets paid by the business. The practice locks in talent while building greater financial stability for the Next-Gen worker.

Some companies, like Aetna, match student loan payments for eligible employees, while others, like Estée Lauder, a global beauty product company, contribute monthly payments toward employees' student loans up to a capped amount. Computer technology company Nvidia, for example, reimburses staff up to $500 per month to a lifetime maximum of $30,000.[19]

This is a great perk and one that helps young professionals get a strong start in their business life.

Have them write as a training activity. Performed on a part-time basis each week (and more frequently during slower periods), this activity allows Next-Gen staffers to contribute content for use in newsletters, websites, and the like while encouraging them to *learn the business*. After all, you can't really write about something that you don't understand.

This practice was used by Bob Ruffolo, CEO of Impact, a marketing company. He wanted to keep his staffers engaged and learning, so he had them produce content and videos for use on the firm's website. Since he instituted the idea, Impact's website traffic is up ten-fold with subscriber numbers up over 130 percent.[20]

You can harness the power of the Next-Gen workforce and improve retention by using these ideas. By including younger employees in the operation of the business, you lessen the risk of their early departure, thus achieving the "stickiness" that you want to feel when making investment decisions in developing the Next-Gen worker.

Of course, the melding of high ambition, emotional intelligence, and Next-Gen inclusiveness comes with great diversity of both thought and background—and that can be a challenge to shape and leverage as well.

Shaping a Diverse Workforce

Last year's societal unrest sparked by George Floyd's death and other racial incidences has placed diversity and inclusion at the top of many CEOs' agendas. That's a good thing. Now, I'm not putting any moral or ethical weight on the notion. It is a fact that fielding a cross-cultural workforce is good for business. It enables you to broaden appeal and gain perspectives that, when used, can provide a competitive edge in the marketplace.

Building a diverse workforce is a choice—not an obligation. However, it is a choice you should make because it enhances business value and helps create indispensability. Including people with varied backgrounds and experiences leads to better thinking; better thinking leads to improved business performance.

Additionally, better things come with a diverse and inclusive workforce, including the following.

Better people. Attractive work settings attract good people. Gain a reputation for hiring a cross-cultural workforce and your business will become one, which people want to be a part of.

Better results. Better people deliver better outcomes. A workplace where staff are heard and valued (regardless of age, race, gender, religion, or sexual orientation) positions you to be able to hire the talent needed to improve performance.

In a recent study, the research and advisory company Gartner reports that "bringing diversity into the workforce is effective at a business level. The difference in employee performance between non-diverse and diverse organizations is 12%."[21]

Improved staff involvement and engagement, fostered through greater inclusiveness, delivers results.

Better decision-making. New ways of thinking and doing come with greater workforce diversity, which opens the door to improvements in decision-making and execution within the organization.

Better access to new markets. The diversity of the global marketplace demands that companies understand customer desires from virtually any place on the planet. A diverse workforce can broaden the customer-base because the more diverse the staff, the wider they cast their nets into the marketplace.

Take the advisory firm Out Leadership, for example. By hosting executive summits, creating talent accelerators, and providing strategic insights for CEOs, the firm seeks to help businesses realize the positive business impacts of LGBT+ inclusion. It's a very large market. Out Leadership estimates the global purchasing power of the global LGBT+ consumer market to be $3.6 trillion.[22]

Better culture. Different thoughts and motivations contribute to creating a kaleidoscope of potential that can be harnessed to create a company culture rich in new levels of energy and originality. It is the culture upon which marketplace indispensability is built.

For instance, the world's largest PC vendor, Lenovo, has constructed its success on a strong foundation of diversity and inclusion. It is one of the only Chinese-based firms to be listed on both the Reputation Institute's Global RepTrak 100 (which highlights the world's most reputable companies in regard to innovation, governance, and citizenship) and the Bloomberg Gender Equality Index (which measures gender equality across internal company statistics, employee policies, external community support and engagement, and gender-conscious product offerings).[23]

With fifty-seven thousand employees in more than sixty countries, Lenovo's very tagline, "Different is better," encapsulates the essence of inclusion. Lenovo drives ideas for growth by engaging staff from an array of vastly diverse backgrounds and perspectives. The company demonstrates that diversity can be used as a lever for success.

These arguments round out my case to implore you to build a diverse and inclusive workforce. Just as important, the benefits provided help establish the characteristics needed to become indispensable to your customers. If you want to enjoy these advantages, though, you need to rethink your existing cultural paradigms and reset them to take advantage of the individual differences that comprise your workforce.

The constantly evolving and globally minded epoch of the early twenty-first-century business world demands that you do.

Of course, as you bring on new and diverse staffers, be sure to hasten their assimilation through deliberate mentorship.

Mentorship Provides the Glue

Doc Schilke and Jim Johnson were my mentors early in my professional life. They gave me the opportunities to show what I could do, and more importantly, they believed in me when others thought I was too young and inexperienced to have the responsibilities that they had entrusted to me.

I like to think that their investment has paid off. By the age of thirty, I had written my first business book and launched a nearly thirty-year consulting career that brings me to writing the very book that you're reading today.

You owe it to your people to provide the mentorship that they need to thrive.

Clearly, Doc and Jim invested quite a bit of themselves to teach, inspire, and guide me. However, I had to take the initiative to build a relationship with both of them. I had to ask them for their support and advice. Not every staffer is willing to take that risk. Of course, I also had to turn the advice that I received from them into action. Not every staffer has the ego to handle that last part either.

That said, we can ease the mentor process a bit by proactively seeking out staffers to mentor. Here are some characteristics to look for.

Desire. Seek out people who want it! Find staff members with fire in their bellies—the ones who want to be the best they can be. They're the people you can mentor.

I was working with a client a while ago who had an irate parent calling the office of the CHRO because their son, let's call him "Little Johnny," had been removed from the firm's mentor program due to a lack of interest. They wanted to schedule a meeting with their son's manager and HR representative to discuss the matter.

While this situation is appalling on so many levels, clearly Little Johnny is not a good candidate for mentorship.

Self-awareness. The best mentoring candidates possess the self-awareness needed to know what they're not so good at. They also tend to possess a kind of reserve that makes them avid learners—exactly the kind of person you want to invest in developing.

In my executive coaching business, I tend to be asked to mentor high-potential individuals—grooming them to one day inherit top leadership spots. Sometimes I get some people who are lacking in self-awareness. These people have the kinds of blind spots that make them very challenging to work with. They tend to be extremely defensive or too ready to withdraw and pout at the first whiff of criticism. They're not the people who should be mentored, and I tend to suggest that to clients who pair them with me.

Modesty. Whenever I needed to be knocked down a peg, my mentors were really good at humbling me. Find people who lack the pretentiousness to resist this kind of coaching and you've got yourself someone worth mentoring.

I still remember all of the red ink that Doc left all over the first draft of my very first business article. He spared me no quarter with his edits. However, the piece was later published in a national magazine. It served as an early launching pad for my young career.

Confidence. The best mentoring candidates must have the requisite confidence to be taught what they need to learn. I'm talking about *true* confidence here, not the false kind that can sometimes be a result of overzealous parents eager to praise their wunderkinds when a good, stiff reality check may be more in order.

Tenacity. There's a lot to be said about the value of *intestinal fortitude*. The best mentor candidates are ones who can stick with mentoring through adversity. Career success is dependent on one's willingness to do whatever it takes to get things done.

Many of the *high potentials* I work with through my coaching work have tenacity baked into their personalities. Often, these people didn't have it easy as children and are determined to turn that around as young professionals.

We have an obligation to mentor the next generation of leaders and help them build a solid foundation for their *business life*. We need to be willing to deliver the right lessons that will propel them forward and help them be ready to lead our organizations tomorrow.

Indispensable Businesses Are Talent Magnets

As we conclude, allow me to submit that to get the "right" people for your business, you must become a talent magnet. You get the *best and brightest* by offering a terrific work experience.

At the risk of repeating myself, here's how you do it:

1. **Craft a compelling and engaging story.** The articulation of a vision, one that people can buy into and see themselves being successful in, is essential in becoming a talent magnet. If people can't see a path to personal success, they are not apt to do all that they can to make your company indispensable. Give them something to believe in!

2. **Be with your people.** Sounds simple enough, but do your people have ample access to your leadership team? If not, promote some walking around. Be among your people. Be seen. Set the example that inspires your people to bust through walls and become indispensable.

   Take Marriott International, for example. It has been reported that on any given day, around lunchtime, eighty-six-year-old executive chairman Bill Marriott finds his way to the cafeteria on the ground floor of the Bethesda, Maryland, headquarters. He picks up a tray, chooses some food, stands in line, and pays for his meal just like any other employee. He then finds a table and has his lunch with anyone who wishes to join him. Despite being the executive chairman and one of the richest people in the country, Bill eschews special treatment. He shows up for lunch, as he does for board meetings, as an ordinary person. When engaging with employees and clients, he brings interest, presence, and care rather than status, hierarchy, and power.[24]

This sets a powerful example for the people of Marriott and demonstrates a behavior that can help you create an indispensable business too.

3. **Play fair.** People want to be treated fairly. Equitably enforcing the rules goes a long way in building a high-trust workplace. Operating procedures and the rules of engagement must be understood by all and carried forth in an unbiased way.

4. **Provide skills and career growth.** Help your people become all that they can be and you'll engage your team in a way that is tough to beat. If people can see themselves getting ahead and achieving their own personal goals, they're likely to stick.

For example, Adobe doesn't use ratings to establish employee capabilities, feeling that this inhibits creativity and harms how teams work. Instead, managers take on the role of a coach, letting employees set goals and determine how they should be assessed.[25]

The approach seems to be working. The company appears on several "Best Places to Work" lists.

5. **Empower and enable independence.** Micromanagement alienates your best staffers.

Warren Buffett, chairman of Berkshire Hathaway, exemplifies the point. Recently, Stanford Graduate School of Business (GSB) professor David F. Larcker and Stanford GSB researcher Brian Tayan surveyed approximately eighty Berkshire subsidiary CEOs, and here's what they said about being empowered by the billionaire: "The CEOs provide monthly financial statements to headquarters, but they have infrequent contact with Buffett. Most report having phone calls with him on a monthly or quarterly basis. None have a pre-established schedule, and all said they initiate the communication themselves."[26]

Who are we to argue with Warren Buffett?

6. **Change things up.** The best workers want to do interesting work. Create opportunities to assign staffers varied and challenging work and watch them grow.

   The Coca-Cola Company, for example, is known for its strong company culture, which features short-term assignments that expose associates to work that is different from what they do on a daily basis. These assignments can be in another country or market or, simply, a *project-based* one that provides an opportunity for professional growth. Regardless, the variety makes for a positive culture at Coke.

7. **Reward and recognize results.** Indeed, we all need some positive reinforcement when we're doing all that we can to deliver results. Be sure to call out and celebrate the people who are making your company indispensable.

8. **Seek balance.** A 24-7 work life leads to burnout. Seek to establish a balance for your people through policy-setting and benefits.

   Defense industry giant Raytheon, for example, places great emphasis on helping employees maintain the proper work-life balance. It offers flexible work schedules, including compressed workweeks, flextime, job-sharing, reduced hours, and telecommuting, along with up to three weeks of paid parental leave and adoption services, designed to offset the out-of-pocket costs associated with adopting a child.[27]

   Clearly, these kinds of programs aren't reserved for Silicon Valley start-ups. Established, old-guard companies like Raytheon can successfully institute them too—and so can you!

To Close

The ways in which you choose to put these elements into place are situational. Work setting, business location, and the nature of the work itself all have an effect on how a business institutes the concepts to make the greatest impact. Job rotation programs, in-house child day care, flextime, tuition reimbursement, mentoring, stock option rewards, and the like are quickly becoming standard fare for companies wishing to be *employers of choice*. Certainly, these kinds of programs can forge the foundation of what I'm suggesting. But more deliberate effort is essential to get the "right" people in place and retain the talent needed to become and remain indispensable.

Empowerment and trust are next on the Indispensable Agenda. We will cover some of the finer points related to those essential elements of indispensability in chapter 6.

Chapter 5's Indispensable Top Ten List

This chapter is loaded with great content and insight. This is a list of the top ten ideas summarized for easy consumption. Be sure to take a deeper dive into other key concepts by reviewing the chapter in detail.

1. Your EVP is of vital importance in attracting and retaining the kind of talent that you need to become indispensable.
2. You can invest in building a dog-friendly skate park right in the middle of your company headquarters and encourage your staff to take a snooze in those fancy nap pods that you bought on Amazon, but none of these so-called engagement devices is the answer to getting and keeping the right people.
3. Place focus on the outside: whether real or imagined, a sense that an "enemy" wants to destroy the company will inspire your people to work together to defeat that adversary. In turn, this will engage your team in the work at hand.
4. When the chips are down, you want people who are hungry for achievement. You want to hire naturally ambitious people.
5. High EQ contributors are priceless to a business because they are habitually modest and unassuming. Indeed, these are the people you need to become indispensable.
6. There is no value more essential to becoming indispensable in the marketplace than putting the customer first.
7. Flip the pyramid if you want to deliver exceptional service all of the time.

8. Form a committee of younger staff and charge them to plan and host events that feature senior leaders discussing important business issues. This activity helps establish a two-way conversation between Next-Gen staff and their top management.

9. Building a diverse workforce is a choice—not an obligation. However, it is a choice you should make because it enhances business value and helps create indispensability.

10. You owe it to your people to provide the mentorship that they need to thrive.

The Right Trust and Empowerment

OUR NEXT AGENDA ITEM REMINDS us to institute the "right" trust and empowerment practices so our companies can become indispensable.

With the right people in place, one would think that trust and empowerment simply go with the territory. However, with all that has transpired in the business world and society in general of late, it's safe to assume that blind trust in those who lead is dwindling, and staffers don't always feel all that engaged or empowered.

Sure, the COVID-19 crisis has many people feeling unsettled about their future. However, that doesn't tell the whole story. There are just too many examples of corruption and cagey behavior to assume that your people will necessarily give you (and the rest of your leadership team) the benefit of the doubt just because you're at the top of the pyramid.

Many are disheartened by the countless examples of corruption and unrest that splash across our collective newsfeeds. From claims that surfaced last year that some U.S. lawmakers used inside information to make money in the stock market as the pandemic first hit our shores to tear-gassed mothers in Portland, Oregon, people are giving up on the notion that a bright and boundless future lies ahead.

Of course, a sense of unease has been building for many years now. However, recent events have exasperated the situation. That said, business leaders must begin to recognize the impact that this has on an organization and understand how it limits your company's potential to become indispensable in the marketplace.

The Symptoms That Indicate You May Be Affected

Here are a few characteristics that can indicate that your workforce may be feeling the pain:

1. **General anxiety:** Undoubtedly, morale and productivity are impacted when staffers feel anxious about their future. If left unchecked, anxiety will impact company performance.

   For example, according to the *Huffington Post*, low employee morale at DISH Network Corporation may be having an impact on the company's bottom line as well as on investor relations.[1] The company's stock price has fallen by roughly 25 percent in the past year.

   With DISH Network's 2019 year-to-date revenue totaling $9.57 billion, compared to $10.31 billion in revenue from the same period last year,[2] the TV satellite provider needs to figure out how to motivate the troops to get its business back on track.

2. **Despondency:** People disconnect from their commitment to the company when feeling hopeless and suspicious of intent. This can be disastrous to a business. You've got to do all that you can to reengage your people or results will suffer.

   Consider Kraft Heinz Company, regularly rated as one of the worst companies to work for.[3] Its CEO Bernardo Hees had to leave his position in 2019 due to the fact that the company wrote down the value of Kraft and Oscar Mayer by $15 billion, reported a $12.6 billion loss for the fourth quarter of 2018, cut its dividends by 36 percent, and announced that its accounting practices are under investigation by the Securities and Exchange Commission.[4]

Kraft Heinz is a solid example of what can happen when staff are disillusioned.

3. **Self-aggrandizement:** This kind of behavior is often reinforced by social media, where posting pictures of the hamburger that you're about to eat is commonplace. Consequently, many people come to work each day with a belief that they deserve to be treated like royalty. When self-promotion replaces teamwork, staff can quickly shift to an "every man for himself" attitude, which stifles growth and hampers results.

   In fact, a recent *Harvard Business Review* article reported on research conducted by Russell Reynolds Associates, in partnership with Hogan Assessment Systems, which found that "intensity, an ability to prioritize and focus on substance, and an ability to know what one doesn't know (and utilize the best in what others do know) are more strongly related to best-in-class CEO leadership than traditional traits like extroversion or self-promotion."[5]

   We need to put the ego in the back seat if we are going to engage and inspire.

4. **Exaggerated self-importance:** Inspired by some of the stories that they see in the media, people in leadership positions can often develop a false sense of their pomposity. This only leads to *no good* as your leaders attempt to gain the privileges that they think they are *owed* by their position.

   Take Steph Korey, the former CEO of luggage manufacturer and retailer Away, who had to step down from her role following a scathing report that detailed allegations of a toxic workplace culture perpetuated by Korey.[6]

   Clearly, she did not behave in ways that garnered trust or fostered an empowered workforce.

5. **Beleaguered leadership:** When company morale is at its lowest, a leader without a clear and consistent message about how the organization will evolve from here to there is discounted by the rank and file. Leaders need to lead and communicate or they're dead in the water.

Nike's CEO Mark Parker had been with the company since 1979 but chose to step down from the helm of the sportswear giant because of multiple lawsuits over alleged gender discrimination and a "boys' club" culture at Nike.[7]

It seems Nike staff was losing faith in its leader.

How to Transcend the Fog of a Low-Trust Workplace

As mentioned at the outset of this book, we have to give people something to believe in! We do that by cultivating a vision of the business that is centered on trust and doing the work needed to build a high-integrity organization that people can depend on both inside and outside of the enterprise.

We've got to enhance the sense of "being in it together" within the business and take the steps outlined earlier to build a sense of community that can energize your team and help them care about each other. By giving them something bigger than themselves to be part of at work, we create a "safe space" for them to be at their best. We need our people to be at their best in order to become indispensable to our customers.

While a feeling of malaise and mistrust may pervade today's society, it doesn't have to be brought to work each day, eroding morale and having a negative impact on performance. Here are some ways to take deliberate action and improve trust within your business:

- Root out and repair trust breakdowns.
- Keep promises.
- Be transparent.
- Embrace the "beatitudes" of high integrity business behavior.

Let's explore each of these important facets of trust-building within an indispensable company.

Root Out and Repair Trust Breakdowns

Trust is a fragile thing. It takes a great amount of time to build; it takes only moments to bust apart.

Incomplete feedback loops and a lack of clarity in decision-making authority in delegation and empowerment and in employee engagement and transparency have the potential to cause breakdowns in trust within an organization.

According to a study quoted in a recent *Harvard Business Review* article, trust can make a huge difference in the way a company executes its mission: "Compared with people at low-trust companies, people at high-trust companies report: 74% less stress, 106% more energy at work, 50% higher productivity, 13% fewer sick days, 76% more engagement, 29% more satisfaction with their lives, 40% less burnout."[8]

Indeed, indispensable companies must be diligent about building *and* maintaining trust—top to bottom and across the business. If you fear that a lack of trust may be killing your business, do something about it! Sponsor a trust program that can repair trust breakdowns.

Here's how:

1. **Determine where your firm lies on the trust maturity curve:** Make an honest assessment about how your team operates. Are they empowered? Do they ask for permission before making a decision? Do you set a solid example of trustworthiness or are you interceding at every turn?

    You do not determine the answer to these questions, though. Your team and staff are responsible for determining where the business is on the curve.

2. **Build a trust framework:** Determined by where you sit on the curve, a set of trust values and operating principles need to be defined and instituted next. Think of the values of the "what" you're looking for and consider the operating principles as the "how."

    For example, a trust value might be "We empower our frontline staff to make customer-facing decisions." Corresponding operating principles would be related to the provision of necessary training and coaching to improve the preparedness of staff to make proper customer support decisions.

3. **Provide trust training:** Trust training needs to be delivered to all levels of the organization. The goal should be to help people explore the subtle ways that trust can erode within a business. By exposing staff to blind spots in their behaviors that can lead to mistrust, you enable them to make adjustments to the way they do things that can improve trust in the organization.

   For example, a leader who fails to address a low performer can lead other members of their team to develop misgivings about whether they can trust that leader to do the "right" thing in other business situations. Proper trust training can help your staff learn how their behavior impacts the *trust quotient* at your firm.

4. **Establish a trust measurement plan and progress milestones:** How do you know if you're making progress? Determine measurement criteria and milestones. These measurements and milestones should center on changes in behaviors up and down the organization. Additionally, polling of staff following the completion of early initiatives is an appropriate way to assess the successful evolution toward building a higher trust culture.

It should be noted that it can take three to four months to get a trust program off the ground. Additionally, it will likely require a small team of four or five people (with some help from outside experts) to get the job done. Nonetheless, once the program is moving, its benefits will be immediately felt as a more empowered and inspired workplace emerges.

Recently, I was working with a client on a trust-building program. We followed the aforementioned steps and, with a small work team comprised of client personnel, were able to deliver a powerful set of *personal action reminders* that we promulgated throughout the firm via its intranet. These *trust prompts*, as we called them, would stream at the bottom of staffer's screens throughout the day, reminding them to practice good trust-building behaviors. Here are just a few of the prompts:

1. Keep promises—if you said it, do it!
2. Listen up—be sure to understand before responding.

3. Talk straight—do not mislead.

4. Address the tough stuff—don't avoid what must be confronted.

5. Fix it—don't let misunderstandings fester.

Not only did trust rise, but the client gained a productivity boost too. It seems that people work better when trust is high. It all begins with keeping promises.

Keep Promises

Keeping promises promotes reliability and fidelity from stem to stern within an enterprise. Therefore, a *leadership team must create a culture that keeps its promises.*

Why?

Your culture determines where the bar of acceptable behavior is set within your business. If you, as a leader, tolerate a culture that doesn't keep its word, you will fail. You will fail because your people will not remain committed to your vision. You will fail because your customers will not receive the service that they demand. You will fail because the marketplace will not respond favorably to a business that can't be trusted.

On the other hand, if you commit to constructing a culture that is dependable and trustworthy, you will succeed. Your people will stay committed. Your customers will feel that they come first. The marketplace will respond in kind.

Consider the meteoric rise of Quicken Loans. One of the ways that it demonstrates its dependability is through the adoption and execution of a nonnegotiable rule: *every customer phone call and email must be returned on the same day that it is received.*[9] Clearly, this policy builds trust among its customers—Quicken Loans is the largest originator of home mortgages in the country.

Of course, trust starts at the top. You and your leadership team must become living examples of trustworthiness. Don't say anything that you don't believe to be true. Stop spinning the facts in your favor. Stomp out any kind of behavior that may erode trust. Adopt a "say what you mean and do what you say" attitude in all of your business affairs.

Quicken Loans founder, Dan Gilbert, sets the example when it comes to emphasizing the firm's same-day return call and return email policy. He goes so far as to give new hires at training sessions his direct-dial extension and tells them, "If you're too busy to" return a customer voice mail, "I'll do it for you."[10]

If you and your leaders can do the same—set the example and operate with high integrity all the time—you will establish a high standard of excellence and honor. Your people will know what "right" looks like. They will know how they are expected to behave.

Build a culture that keeps promises, explicit and implied. It's as simple as that.

Be Transparent

There is no doubt that outstanding things happen when people who work together trust each other.

Yes, your business is sure to face adversity. It's part of the equation. Trust serves as a ballast against adversity. Do you want your team to address problems head-on? Do you want them to do their best and make no excuses for less-than-optimal performance? Do you want them to pull together when confronted with unforeseen challenges? You'd best build a high-trust work environment for your people to thrive in or just forget about being indispensable.

Trust-building begins with open, honest, and transparent communication. Where to start? Here are four steps that you can take to begin the journey of establishing a transparent communications culture within your company:

1. **Make it a priority:** Don't just talk about becoming transparent. Insist on transparency. Be clear and deliberate about it. Be sure that your top leadership understands your intent.

   When the leadership team at GDLS decided to make transparent communications a *strategic thrust* within their business transformation strategy, they gave it a name: *Communicate with Purpose*.

By giving it a name and reinforcing it through action, the firm's leadership were making transparency a priority.

2. **Solicit opinions and gain insights:** With the intent well understood, it's time to assess where your communications practices stand in regard to transparency. Tap a good cross-section of suppliers, distributors, customers, and staff for their impressions on the firm's communication. Ask questions about the frequency, quality, effectiveness, variety, and most decisively, the integrity of the communications that your company generates. This exercise provides necessary perspective. It will indicate where issues may lie. It will be the fodder needed for change.

   For example, we surveyed staff and customers alike during my work with Mitsui Sumitomo Insurance. The input received was instrumental in identifying areas needing the utmost attention. Perhaps the most interesting set of findings came from the customer survey. It was through that lens that we were able to recognize the importance of equipping frontline staff with better systems so they could then disseminate accurate information to agents and insureds.

3. **Describe what it looks like:** Using the gathered perspectives as a backdrop, the next step involves defining, as completely as possible, exactly "what" you want that transparent communications environment to look like, including details about

   - the transparency ethos to be instituted,
   - the ways that you and your people communicate transparently,
   - expected communication behaviors, and
   - communications principles related to content, frequency, style, stakeholder expectations, and areas of communication responsibilities.

   The LexisNexis vision story contained an entire section on transparent communications. It promoted the need and it described a target work setting that the company was thriving to realize, including guiding principles (which we called *strategic guideposts*) and details on expected behaviors.

For example, one of the ten strategic guideposts read, "We will focus on cascading strategic communication to all employees to drive change and increase employee engagement."

Complete with its rationale and set of implications, this principle set the stage for many communication improvement initiatives that have since been taken on by the company.

4. **Craft the plan:** It's here that you change words into action. Build a plan that delineates all of the follow-up activities to be done in order to institutionalize a transparent communications environment within the business.

There was an entire communications program developed at GDLS as the result of its transformation effort. Highlights include work aimed at improving union communication, field personnel training, and expanding multichannel communication mechanisms to ensure that staff, customers, and suppliers get the information that they need in the ways and means that they like to receive it.

GDLS serves as a terrific example of how a company can shift its culture to achieve greater transparency.

Remember, it's our responsibility to establish a transparent communications culture. It is also our job to act and communicate transparently ourselves, for greater transparency breeds greater integrity. After all, we model the behaviors that our staffers adopt. We define "how to be" to make our organizations indispensable.

With that, here are a few ideas for driving high-integrity behavior within your business.

The "How to Be's" to Drive Integrity

Adopt these practices and help your colleagues operate with exceptional integrity while establishing better trust within your workplace:[11]

1. **Be real, for it inspires confidence:** Authenticity and integrity go hand in hand. Being real gives you legitimacy. It helps others to

know that you're sincere in your words and actions. People trust people who keep it real. And no one likes, or trusts, someone who is disingenuous.

The research backs it up. A study conducted by University of Nebraska professors Susan Jensen and Fred Luthans showed that authentic leadership serves as the single strongest predictor of an employee's job satisfaction, organizational commitment, and workplace happiness.[12]

So be sure to keep it real as you drive your business to indispensability.

2. **Be clear, for it limits confusion:** They say that curiosity killed the cat. Let me suggest that ambiguity can kill the business. Don't beat around the bush. Let others know where you're coming from. While some leaders may like to operate under a cloud of uncertainty, thinking that it keeps people on their toes, this type of behavior only leads to mistrust. Instead, be the truth-teller and no one will doubt your honesty.

Consider how Dr. Anthony Fauci rose to prominence during the COVID-19 outbreak. While not without his critics, Fauci helped gain the trust of a vast majority of the American people by providing an honest assessment of the ever-changing situation, often needing to *face down* political pressure to do otherwise.

Indeed, truth-telling and clarity of message build trust even in uncertain times.

3. **Be accountable, for it demonstrates reliability:** As discussed earlier, keeping your word and taking responsibility radiates integrity and brings about trust. When things get tough, your team will know that you are someone they can count on and believe in.

Bill George writes about the need for accountability in leadership in his book *Discover Your True North* when describing how Anne Mulcahy began the turnaround at Xerox, just after she was named its CEO. He writes, "Instead of endless rounds of meetings at headquarters, Mulcahy visited customers' offices and rode with field salespeople to see whether she could help stem the tide of customer defections and field-sales resignations. She told the sales force, 'I will go anywhere, anytime, to save a Xerox customer.' Her customer engagement contrasted sharply with that of her predecessor, who rarely traveled outside headquarters. It sent an important signal that solidified the Xerox field organization and restored customer confidence."[13]

Mulcahy's action showed her team and her customers that she was a leader who could be counted on.

4. **Be respectful, for it precipitates respect:** Demonstrating respect for others is an essential element of integrity. It is often a forgotten part of building trust as well. But respectfulness earns the confidence of others. Once confidence is established, trust follows.

5. **Be humble, for it personifies integrity:** Humility helps others see your humanity. Being unpretentious helps people learn to trust you. Practice humility and people will flock to follow you.

    However, fake humility won't get you very far. I once worked with a young man who used humility as a tool to manipulate people. He'd use the "Oh, golly shucks, you're so much more experienced and intelligent than I'll ever be" routine to encourage people to let down their guard and initially trust him. But as soon as they disagreed with his point of view, the humility routine went out the door, and in came the overconfident egotist who had an insatiable need to always be the smartest guy in the room. Needless to say, he failed once his people got hip to his act.

6. **Be an exceptional listener, for it expresses caring:** Listening carefully is part of operating with high integrity. Seeking understanding of what a person means (and not just what they're saying) will forge stronger connections with them. The better you listen, the more you show you care.

7. **Be a continuous learner, for it enables you to teach:** High integrity individuals help others become stronger. The more that you learn, the better equipped you are to teach others. People come to trust others who are helpful. Learn and teach and you will embody a person worthy of trust.

Charles Brindamour is the CEO of Intact Financial Corporation, the largest provider of property and casualty insurance in Canada. Brindamour exemplifies the point. It has been reported that when Brindamour became CEO of Intact, he blocked out three to four hours every morning to gain a better understanding of areas that could influence his company or the lives of his employees.

"Learning to have perspective on things is really important. It's never all black or white," he said in an interview, adding, "If you don't make this a priority, you risk the organization becoming complacent."[14]

8. **Be a great example, for it inspires change:** If you want to weave high integrity into your company's DNA, show others what a person who can be trusted looks like. Be the person who garners trust through your candor, earnestness, honesty, and integrity, and watch others model your behavior.

Consider José Mujica, Uruguay's former president. After getting elected as the president in 2009, he donated all of his money to charity and shunned an opulent presidential mansion to live a life of simplicity on a farm with his wife.[15] Consequently, his administration was able to bring about tremendous social change, including the legalization of marijuana, gay marriage, and abortion—all this in an overwhelmingly conservative, Roman Catholic country.

Once you have established a culture of trust and high integrity, you're positioned to enable your people to become self-sufficient.

Here are some thoughts on how to build a self-sufficient workforce.

Fostering Self-Sufficiency

If your team lacks what it takes to perform at the highest level without your guidance, your company will never be able to become indispensable in the marketplace. How can it, when your people are dependent on you (or someone else, for that matter) to lead the way?

You must be certain that your people have what it takes to get the job done—even when you're not there to direct them. Here are a few simple steps to take to foster self-sufficiency within your organization:

1. **Show them:** People need to know what *good* looks like to be self-sufficient. Show them. Provide clear and concise instructions on how to get the job done right the first time.

   You can help less experienced team members get up-to-speed by pairing them with a more experienced staffer, who can show them the ropes while providing tips and techniques for delivering exceptional results.

2. **Set the standard:** Just like setting the expectation for a child to make their own bed every day, you need to define the goals, objectives, and expected outcomes for your people to achieve or run the risk that the work won't get done at the right level of proficiency.

   Steve Jobs, for example, is a leader who set the expectation bar very high. But his work ethos helped Apple colleagues design and build products for the mass market, which elevated Apple from a niche product company to an industry disruptor.

3. **Stay connected:** With the goals set, it is still important to make your presence known. Besides using customary performance-monitoring techniques like reviewing production reports and the like, make a call or take a stroll around and check in on your people as they're doing their jobs. It's a great way to stay connected and see where you can add additional value and make your team stronger.

   Like many businesses during the pandemic, the management team at Vertafore, an insurance agency software vendor, used Zoom as a way to stay connected with staffers. Besides holding weekly meetings, managers were encouraged to schedule *virtual happy hours*, featuring games like *Name That Tune* and *Trivial Pursuit* as a means of showing frontline personnel that they cared.

   Self-sufficiency improves when people feel cared for and looked after.

4. **Coach, but don't do:** Like doting parents who just can't help but make the bed for their kids, at the first signs of trouble, some managers can't seem to resist getting down into the weeds and doing the work of their team by themselves.

   Please resist that urge. It's not good for anyone involved. Instead, reinforce through coaching. It helps build self-sufficiency and confidence.

   WAIT is an expression used in executive coaching circles. The acronym stands for *Why Am I Talking.* I use it quite often with the executives and emerging leaders whom I coach. It serves as an effective way to remind them of the importance of listening and resisting the urge to dominate a conversation or take over a situation they should otherwise let their teams handle.

   I offer this to you so that the next time you feel the need to hijack a situation at work, just *WAIT*!

5. **Readily recognize, and only reward when appropriate:** Your team is supposed to be doing a good job all of the time. Readily acknowledge their good performance. As noted earlier, people want to feel appreciated. However, reserve rewards and resounding recognition for those times when exceptional effort was needed or all of your expectations were wildly exceeded.

   In this way, your team can learn the difference between good and great.

   It is, indeed, in your best interest to help your team become self-sufficient. It is only through self-sufficiency that true empowerment comes. You need an empowered workforce to become indispensable.

How to Institutionalize Empowerment

As we round out this chapter, it's important to note that research suggests the best way to motivate your people is to create a work setting that enables empowerment.

More specifically, the research attributed the perception of one's *free will* as a significant predictor of personal achievement. The researchers concluded through their study that our motivation can be accelerated when we believe that we're in control of results, and our motivation wanes when it is believed that *outside influencers* can impact outcomes.[16]

Based on the research, it would seem that we get the best business results when our work settings make people feel empowered. Of course, you just can't wave a magic wand and make people empowered. Empowerment requires proper preparation.

Here is a checklist to consider when working on institutionalizing empowerment within your company:

1. **Readiness:** Are they ready to be empowered? As mentioned earlier, staff members need to be ready to take on greater responsibility. Are they properly trained? Do they have the requisite experience? If not, you must prepare your people to be empowered before you award them the responsibility of self-management. Once they're ready, let them drive decision-making.

   Zappos, for example, does an outstanding job cultivating its "customer first" culture by providing its frontline staff with the necessary training needed to bestow upon them the decision-making power to *wow* the customer.

2. **Expectations:** Do they understand the expected results? Once your staff is ready to be empowered, you must set expectations for business outcomes. If they don't understand your expectations, you can't expect them to make the *right* call. Be sure that your team knows your intent before you unleash them on the world.

3. **Controls:** Can you measure and monitor performance? You'll want to be sure that there are appropriate measures and controls in place to verify the quality of the work as it is performed.

   Of course, technology can help.

   For example, when working with The Hartford to improve its claim-handling processes a few years ago, we instituted an AI-based tool to help claims-handling staff lower their total cost per case (TCPC)—a key measurement of claim-handler effectiveness.

This system helped reduce claim-handler dependency on supervisory review and sign-off by flagging only the cases that needed supervisory review because of out-of-range results (based on the embedded predictive analytics of the system). Within a year of systems implementation, the firm's TCPC decreased by nearly 15 percent, and customer satisfaction (as measured by postclaim settlement surveys) improved by more than 10 percent.

The Hartford enabled staff empowerment and enhanced adherence to process standards while improving personnel execution and customer satisfaction with technology.

4. **Decision rights:** Do they know which decisions they're not authorized to make? There will always be some decisions that require your review and input. Of course, a delicate balance must be struck. Should you intervene too much, you will sabotage your empowerment agenda—not enough, and you will assume needless business risk. It's essential that your *decision rights* are clearly defined and understood across your team. Be sure staffers understand when to escalate issues to you and when to *make the call* on their own.

5. **Presence:** Are you present and part of the operation? A leader of an empowered team still has a role to play among his or her people. Your presence must be felt, if for no other reason than to inspire confidence among your players.

Jim Johnson was a mentor of mine. He came at the "right" time in my career—that critical early point when I needed someone to remind me that it was OK to be successful. Jim was a vice president and thought leader at the Equitable Life (known as AXA Equitable Insurance Company today). Jim was a master of this style of empowered leadership.

Like a walking Serenity Prayer, Jim had the sense to accept the things he could not change, the courage to change the things he could, and the wisdom to know the difference. He was probably the only guy on the planet to be foolish enough to give a twenty-four-year-old an opportunity to be one of his assistant vice presidents.

His coaching made a huge difference in my professional life. He was there to guide me through the challenges that came from leading a team of professionals as its youngest member. He was there to guide me as a part of a senior leadership team whose members were, on average, fifteen years my senior. I wrote my first book thirty years ago, in part, with encouragement from Jim.

It's up to us, as leaders, to create and cultivate the work settings required to empower our people to achieve and gain the buoyancy to be self-sufficient, like Jim Johnson did for me.

To Close

As discussed throughout the book, the best teams are made of members who have each other's backs. They care for one another. They look out for each other. They're unselfish. This chapter reminds us that trust and empowerment are essential underpinnings of the kind of "team first" culture that is so essential to building an indispensable enterprise.

Of course, this doesn't happen by accident. Rather, it is built over time from the top down. As we close the chapter, here are ten tips that you can follow to establish a high-trust, deeply empowered work environment:

1. **Take the blame.** Sometimes your team will not succeed. Take the blame for the failure and move on. This builds trust in you and inspires your team to never let you down again.

   For example, Starbucks CEO Kevin Johnson took accountability when a Philadelphia Starbucks store manager overreacted by having two black men arrested for loitering. He didn't fire the manager. Instead, he closed his stores for a day of racial bias training, offered to personally mentor the two men who were arrested—Rashon Nelson and Donte Robinson—and helped them complete their bachelor's degrees.[17]

2. **Enable self-sufficiency.** Help your people be the best that they can be by showing them how to become self-sufficient.

3. **Be transparent.** Share information about the business and its strategies before your people fill the information vacuum with theories, conjecture, and misinformation.

   PepsiCo, for example, began sharing its problems regarding its distribution channels and product mix with its unionized drivers. Interestingly, once the drivers understood the issues, they were able to contribute insights and ideas for improvement that were just as good as any that could have come from a team of management consultants.[18]

4. **Be empathetic.** Demonstrate your willingness to understand and open a dialogue that builds trust and encourages workplace excellence.

   In a recent Inc.com article, Rana el Kaliouby, cofounder and CEO of Affectiva, an emotion measurement technology company that grew out of MIT's Media Lab, wrote, "I'm encouraging my team to carve out time—and literally block it on their calendars—throughout the day to spend time with family, help kids with e-learning, check in on elderly relatives, and, crucially, take time for self-care. We all respect those blocks on one another's calendars, even if it's somewhat 'disruptive' to a normal course of business. I myself have been trying to block time to help my son with online learning. We need to be flexible with ourselves and those around us."[19]

   It serves as an amazing example of leadership empathy that arose during the onset of the pandemic. It demonstrates how a leader can understand what their people are up against and take appropriate action to help calm the situation.

5. **Fix a wrong.** Don't allow strained work relationships to worsen beyond repair. Instead, take the steps necessary to set things right.

   A recent survey by Weber Shandwick, one of the world's leading communications and marketing services firms, shines a light on the point. They found the following:[20]

   - 87 percent of workers indicated that workplace incivility has an impact on work performance.
   - 55 percent of respondents said their morale suffered.

- 45 percent expressed a desire to quit.
- 38 percent felt anger toward coworkers or the employer.
- 36 percent noticed a reduction in the quality of their work.
- 33 percent discouraged others from working at the company.
- 32 percent experienced a negative effect on their personal time.
- 26 percent felt less creative.
- 23 percent called in sick.

Clearly, you can't become indispensable in the marketplace if your work environment allows bad behavior to impact performance.

6. **Own your mistakes.** Show your team that you're not infallible. Own up to your mistakes and show how you're taking actions to correct them. This serves as a great example for others to follow, and it builds trust in the workplace.

7. **Give kudos.** As referenced previously, regularly thank your team for the good work that they do. Be sure to give credit where credit is due.

I can still recall the smile on the face of a Mitsui Sumitomo Insurance staffer when Koji Yoshida, the CEO of the insurer's U.S. division, stopped her in the hallway and congratulated her on the delicate handling of a multimillion-dollar catastrophic loss claim suffered by a key customer.

From her expression, you could immediately see how proud she felt that the CEO knew who she was and was willing to stop her in the hallway, in front of her coworkers, to say thank you.

It's proof positive that sometimes trust and empowerment can be built with just a small gesture.

8. **Come clean when you're uncertain.** No need to be a hero. Your team doesn't expect that you have all the answers all of the time. Let them know when you're uncertain and they'll come to trust and respect you even more as a result.

9. **Encourage *esprit de corps*.** Encourage open and honest dialogue within the team. Let people express their discontent. Let them share ideas without the risk of being judged. This is how you build trust and enable empowerment.

On any given day, you're likely to see Gordon Stein, VP of Supply at GDLS, having lunch in the manufacturer's employee lunchroom. This is one of the ways that Stein demonstrates his commitment to practicing an open-door policy. Anyone can pull up a chair, sit down, share a bite, and have a conversation with a senior leader.

10. **Commit to excellence.** Don't settle for second best. Strive for perfection and you will set the foundation on which indispensability can endure.

I hope that you consider using these ten tips when establishing your highly trusting, genuinely enabled, and empowered workforce.

Our last Indispensable Agenda item—change management practices—is covered in the next chapter. These pave the way for even richer and longer-lasting impact when building an indispensable business.

Chapter 6's Indispensable Top Ten List

Here is a list of the top ten takeaways that can be drawn from this chapter. Be sure to take a deeper dive into other key concepts by reviewing the chapter in detail.

1. With all that has transpired in the world as of late, it's safe to assume that blind trust in those who lead is dwindling, and staffers don't always feel all that engaged or empowered.

2. Undoubtedly, morale and productivity are affected when staffers feel anxious about their future.

3. When company morale is at its lowest, a leader without a clear and consistent message about how the organization will evolve from here to there is discounted by the rank and file.

4. Trust is a fragile thing. It takes a great amount of time to build; it takes only moments to bust apart.

5. Keeping promises promotes reliability and fidelity from stem to stern within an enterprise.

6. Transparent communication helps build trust. Don't just talk about becoming transparent. Insist on transparency.

7. Demonstrating respect for others is an essential element of integrity. It is often a forgotten part of trust-building.

8. You must be certain that your people have what it takes to get the job done—even when you're not there to direct them.

9. Research suggests the best way to motivate your people is to create a work setting that enables empowerment.

10. Encourage open and honest dialogue within the team. Let people express their discontent. Let them share ideas without the risk of being judged. This is how you build trust and enable empowerment.

The Right Change Management Practices

OUR LAST AGENDA ITEM IS a discussion of the "right" change management practices. It is a terrific way to tie together all the finer points introduced in earlier chapters, for each point requires just the "right" kind of change management to work.

That said, let's use this chapter as a gentle reminder that not everyone is *wired* like us. In fact, any one of the ideas offered in this book may already be "a bridge too far" for leaders of lesser ilk.

For this reason, the adoption of the "right" change management practices is not only necessary for successful implementation of new ideas, but it is an essential element of becoming indispensable.

Putting the Appropriate Change Practices in Place

Organizations have to change just to remain vital. Some say that they change every day. I'm not sure how much they change day-to-day. However, I do know that the vast majority of organizations require "big changes" if they want to become indispensable. I also know that big changes require a good deal of time. Consequently, proper preparation is required.

Here are six steps that you can take to ensure that your indispensability-driven change framework stands the test of time:

1. **Call it out:** Indispensability efforts deserve a name. So give them one. Identify the specific improvement opportunities that you want to exploit and describe the expected results. This will help others know your intent and begin to identify what's needed to achieve it.

    GDLS' transformation effort was named Vision 2020. Staffers would refer to all of the change initiatives that comprised the program as "Vision 2020 Projects." It made for an easy way to distinguish transformation projects from any other initiatives that were underway.

2. **Take ownership:** Demonstrate "true" executive sponsorship for the effort by identifying yourself as the sponsor of the change program. Your job will be to pave the way for your transformation team and levy the *political clout* needed to garner the right level of participation among stakeholders.

    Early into the GDLS transformation program, we instituted a policy that required each change project to have an executive sponsor from the ranks of the fourteen vice presidents who made up the top leadership team at the company. This ensured executive involvement and demonstrated leadership commitment to the work at hand.

3. **Make it full-time:** Identify a core team that can dedicate a full-time effort to get the job done. This work is too important to be done on a part-time basis. Led by a program manager, it will be the team's responsibility to do the work needed to analyze, discover, and recommend a plan to institute the transformational results needed to make change happen.

    I was made the project manager of the Vision 2020 effort at GDLS. Two of my associates joined me, and a full-time team of four company staffers rounded out the team. Together we drove the transformation planning program for the company.

4. **Engage everyone:** Big change doesn't happen without everyone rowing in the right direction. It requires the involvement and participation of all the firm's staff—top to bottom. Be sure to get key influencers involved early in the effort. Their participation serves to

enlist others. Use interviews, surveys, and workshops to give lower-level staff a voice in the process too.

The GDLS engagement included all of the previous practices. We did one-on-one interviews with each of the fourteen top leaders. We held several workshops that included more than fifty mid-level leaders in the firm. We conducted a companywide survey of employees. These served to gain valuable insights and involve everyone in the change effort.

5. **Determine the path forward:** Once you know the scope of the effort and who needs to participate, it's time to craft a program plan that identifies the projects needed to staff, fund, and execute the vision of indispensability. A published plan helps better manage expectations within the organization.

   Our team at GDLS landed on an initial set of eighteen change projects. They spanned the gamut of size and scope, including projects aimed at improving the customer experience, enhancing internal communications, driving workforce engagement, redesigning process for optimization, and leveraging automation to spur on growth.

6. **Broadcast results:** Be sure to create communication and engagement mechanisms to keep all of your people in the loop. Every one of your staffers need to understand where the firm is in its transformation effort. Be sure to share progress and broadcast results. As outlined in the previous chapter, this promotes transparency and inspires trust within the business.

   The roll-out plan at GDLS included the use of intranet sites, newsletters, and a series of "lunch 'n' learn" meetings as a means to generate enthusiasm, maintain interest, and promote understanding.

   As discussed in chapter 3, you can even choose to regularly produce and distribute a magazine containing articles about project statuses and results. Be sure to fortify it by embedding pictures and pull quotes from staffers involved in the program. This goes a long way in keeping people interested and involved.

Indeed, there's a lot to implementing the changes needed when establishing indispensability, especially because it puts your business in a state of perpetual revitalization.

Indispensability Means Perpetual Revitalization

Once you begin down the road to indispensability, you don't want to let up on the gas pedal. Sure, your business has been successful, but we all know that past results do not guarantee continued success. Regular renewal will be needed to get to your destination—leading to a company that customers can't live without.

Here are some tips that can help you avoid falling into the *comfort zone* and ignore the urge to rest on your laurels:

1. **Recommit to your vision:** Just when you thought it was OK to take a break, it's time to review and recommit to your vision. Determine which products and services are your winners and double down on those. Determine the *Dogs* that just don't align with your strategic intent anymore and divest them. You need to stay focused on the long game to get to indispensability in the marketplace.

   German industrial icon Siemens AG has been in a state of perpetual revitalization since Joe Kaeser took over as its CEO in 2013. Here's a selection of the steps they have taken as reported by Bloomberg:[1]

   - May 2014: Siemens slims its divisions to nine from sixteen, carves out health care, and announces listing of hearing-aid business
   - September 2014: Siemens sells stake in kitchen and washing machine business to Bosch
   - November 2014: Sells hearing-aid unit to EQT for 2.14 billion euros ($2.4 billion)
   - June 2016: Announces merger of wind power division to form Siemens Gamesa
   - May 2019: Siemens announces plan to carve out power and gas businesses

The approach appears to be working. Siemens stock has outpaced GE (the company's chief rival) by more than 80 percent since Kaeser became CEO.

2. **Check alignment:** Is the organizational design aligned with where your company is heading? If not, fix it. Position your best people in places where they can make an impact. Leverage your talent pool by focusing them on tomorrow's growth initiatives. It keeps them fresh and focused, and it delivers what you need to succeed.

3. **Right-size your support areas:** Business support areas that don't directly generate revenue like IT, marketing, HR, and finance often don't get the attention that they deserve. But you need them to achieve your goals. It's essential to reinvigorate these important areas, too, by retooling their processes and ensuring that staff members possess the skills and competencies needed to support future growth.

4. **Renew talent:** With your organization finely tuned, this is a perfect time to lose any dead weight that you may be carrying and renew the talent base with energetic people with fresh ideas.

   GE was notorious for doing this when Jack Welch was its CEO. It was called the "rank and yank" system. For decades, he and his leadership team would annually group staff into three categories—top performers, underperformers, and normal employees. The top performers comprised the top 20 percent of employees and were rewarded, and the bottom 10 percent were labeled underperformers—the underperformers were let go to allow room for hiring new talent.

   The process worked. GE was a recognized leader in all of the industries in which it competed while under Welch.

5. **Promote desired behavior:** The best way to evolve is to measure and reward the behaviors needed to deliver results. Indispensable businesses can't afford to reward effort. Place laser-like focus on outcomes and watch how staffers change the ways in which they operate.

   IBM introduced an app-based performance review system called Checkpoint. It replaced IBM's traditional performance evaluation system, Personal Business Commitments, which was in place for more than a decade.

The app tracks the following five dimensions of employee performance:[2]

- business results,
- impact on client success,
- innovation,
- personal responsibility to others, and
- skills development.

Besides supporting year-end performance reviews, the app enables management and staff to establish a more regular dialogue throughout the year with discussions on shorter-term goals and feedback scheduled through the app on a quarterly basis.

This is a wonderful example of innovative ways businesses are ensuring strategic alignment of their performance systems with their thirst for improved business outcomes.

6. **Promote resilience:** Create a workplace where your people take care of themselves and each other. After all, it takes a team to become indispensable. A winning team needs a culture that enables each player to perform at their best.

The pandemic has shined a spotlight on the issue of resiliency too. Many people have had trouble overcoming the anxiety that comes with the uncertainty of the times. In fact, the CDC published a brief last year, *Employees: How to Cope with Job Stress and Build Resilience during the COVID-19 Pandemic*. It outlined a set of tips for recognizing and managing stress and listed where to go if you needed help.[3]

We will discuss resiliency in more detail later in the chapter—for now, just note that resiliency is a foundation stone of perpetual revitalization, and it needs to be a deliberate part of your cultural dynamic to become indispensable.

7. **Push for "sticky":** Customers "stick" with indispensable businesses because indispensable businesses understand and anticipate their

customer's gravest concerns and challenges and offer solutions that address them. Push for stickiness as you go about revitalizing your business and you'll begin to see ways to become indispensable.

Amazon is a trailblazer when it comes to stickiness. From Amazon Pay, which makes for seamless checkout, to Amazon Prime, which provides free and faster deliveries on online orders and exclusive access to Amazon videos, e-books, and music streaming services, the e-tailer never loses sight of the need make their customers' buying experiences simple and stress-free—making them "stick" as a result.

All of these ideas are ways top leadership can regularly renew their companies.

Deconstructing silos within your business is another important aspect of keeping things fresh and ensuring that your customer never suffers from your company's outdated operating models. Let's look at what is required to institute a different way to organize and manage work.

Remove Silos and Work as One[4]

As businesses grow, they tend to build organizational structures that support larger staff sizes. Larger staffs lead to role specialization. Unfortunately, with more complex organizational designs come the greater likelihood that corresponding governance models divide responsibilities along artificial organizational boundaries. It is this bifurcation of responsibilities that creates a "silo effect" that serves to separate, rather than integrate, the core functions that comprise a business.

If allowed to evolve and extend unencumbered, functional area silos lead to the kind of bureaucracy where hand-offs and bottlenecks get in the way of results. This, in turn, creates a business that is sluggish in response to market changes and unresponsive to emerging opportunities.

Undoubtedly, you don't want silos to take root in your business! It will corrupt your ability to become indispensable. In fact, if silos have already sprouted in your organization, you must weed them out.

Here are some steps that you can take to get started:

1. **Commence transformation programs with indispensability in mind.** Why do we need to break down silos? Ultimately, it all comes down to one thing: *becoming better positioned for indispensability.*

   Of course, the work of breaking down the silos and replacing them with something far more efficient and effective will take some time. After all, these weren't built in a day and they can't come tumbling down in twenty-four hours either.

   That said, it's best to adopt a long-term perspective—one that lets you approach the work at hand in an organized and thoughtful way; one that will not disrupt the work of the business while you're transforming the way you execute.

   As mentioned earlier in the chapter, Siemens AG's CEO Joe Kaeser has forged a mind-set to make his company indispensable, and his adoption of a long-view outlook for driving transformation has delivered great results since he took the helm—that is, if stock prices are any indication.

2. **Identify pain points first.** Once the transformation program begins, survey where work is breaking down. Chances are high that this is happening on the borders of functional area silos. Use this baseline to help you determine your starting point and inform your plan of attack.

3. **Go where the bottlenecks live.** Bottlenecks cause work slowdowns and inhibit performance. Once you know where you want to begin, determine where the bottlenecks exist within the business areas that you're working on at the moment. Fixing these will help you establish some needed momentum at the beginning of your transformation effort.

Pratt & Whitney, a large jet engine manufacturer, went after the bottlenecks through a transformation program aimed at finding and fixing root causes of supplier lead-time problems, pushed to reduce production line rework, and took links out of the distribution chain in an effort to improve factory throughput.

The ongoing transformation effort is making a difference. In June of 2019, Pratt & Whitney announced it has surpassed 17,500 engine deliveries, including auxiliary power units (APUs), to power aircraft for Airbus and its partners, subsidiaries, and joint venture companies. The milestone comes as a result of the production ramp-up in Pratt & Whitney GTF engine deliveries to support the Airbus A320neo and A220 programs.[5]

4. **Identify where the hand-offs are made.** Workflow analysis starts next. To optimize workflow, you need to understand how work is passed from one functional area to the next. The elimination of hand-offs provides opportunities to introduce efficiencies through process redesign and is a great place to introduce software and technology in support of the business.

5. **Create flatter, team-based organizational structures.** Once staff members are thinking differently about how work is done, you can introduce ultramodern organizational designs. Team-based structures, for example, are an emerging trend in business today. This type of organizational design serves to commingle various disciplines into teams. These multidiscipline teams become the work units that replace the silos. When done right, team-based organizational structures improve performance and optimize productivity.

Deloitte's 2019 Global Human Capital Trends survey backs the assertion. Here are some interesting findings from the Deloitte survey:[6]

- 31 percent of respondents indicated that they were almost completely a team/network-based organization.
- 53 percent reported significant performance improvement from the move to a team/network-based structure.

- High-performing organizations are more than twice as likely as their low-performing counterparts to be team-based and include overall team performance in their evaluations.

It seems the only barrier to trading silos for teams is mind-set.

6. **Think "boundaryless!"** As your transformation to indispensability evolves and moves through the organization, it is important to replace command and control thinking with the notion of "boundaryless" process flow. Boundaryless process designs are independent of organization design and physical location. This type of thinking opens the door to innovative ways of reimagining the workplace.

Boundarylessness is so fundamental to indispensability that today's best businesses, including Amazon, FedEx, and Apple, have already rethought their business processes with absolutely no boundaries in mind. By doing so, these businesses have stomped out any remnants of the "it ain't my job" mind-set. Here's how it was done:

1. Teaching managers how to **manage business processes in ways that optimize results** rather than managing the activities of people performing the work

2. Redefining and **reclassifying jobs to match the way work is performed**, ensuring that all associated responsibilities and commitments related to performing the "whole job" are folded into job specifications

Obviously, functional area silos are wildly inefficient and often disruptive to business performance. They must be identified and broken down. It's the only path to indispensability. Otherwise, needless overhead and bureaucracy get in the way of delighting the customer.

Reimagining How Work Gets Done

Reimagining the way work gets done is no small task. It requires a willingness to toss out preconceived notions of how the business operates and necessitates the survey, adjustment, or jettison of jobs that don't align fully with your pursuit of indispensability.

Keep in mind, I'm talking about job elimination, not necessarily the laying off of personnel. After all, you might have the right people, you just might be having them do the wrong things. We can't let job role definitions and boundaries obstruct performance. To do otherwise is to sabotage your efforts of becoming indispensable.

Rather, it's essential that your people understand what's needed next from them so that they can begin to help you rethink the best way to get things done. If you manage to do this, you will have engaged your frontline in redefining their roles and responsibilities. This furthers trust and garners commitment.

Here are three ways that I've helped clients reimagine their work-settings:

1. **Place a focus on people excellence:** Survey leaders at all levels of your organization and ask them one simple question: *Do you have the right people in the right places to do what must be done?* The mere fact that you've asked will prompt good discussions. Those discussions will begin to define alternative ways to organize and leverage your staffers.

   The pandemic, as dreadful as it has been for business, did provide companies with the opportunity to examine this question. As a result of having to work remotely, one of my clients determined that their customer support personnel not only could deliver excellent service from the comfort of their own homes but could improve their productivity by working remotely.

   When their offices officially reopened, the customer support staff was asked to remain working remotely. As a result, they are in the process of renegotiating office leases across their many locations because they have simply reduced their need for workspace.

2. **Place the focus on process excellence:** The next time your team is confronting a thorny business issue, push them to reconsider how to best make good on your value proposition. If you're supposed to deliver fast turnaround, have them look for ways to be faster. If the core value is quality, reinforce that, and drive them to identify

ways to get better. This can be the start of pushing people out of their comfort zones and refocusing them on better ways to get work done.

I've seen this approach work brilliantly at a recent client.

Postmerger, my client was struggling to work as "one." They had been immediately confronted by both internal and external cultural challenges. Intense interest from headquarter representatives from overseas introduced another level of complexity to an already challenging situation.

I urged the leadership team to begin to walk around and talk with their people about how work was done and solicit their ideas for doing it better. The approach worked. The focus shifted away from the "differences" that existed and matured to how to get the job done with an integrated team. The result was new process designs and appropriately redefined job roles and responsibilities.

3. **Place a focus on technology excellence:** Be on a constant lookout for automation and digital capabilities that take the guesswork out of doing the job. The more you can equip your people with the high-end tools they need to deliver, the more flexibility you'll build into the way you're organized and the way you work.

The aforementioned client upgraded their customer support staff's computing capabilities during the pandemic too. They issued laptops with greater processing capabilities than their office desktops and they implemented Microsoft Teams to enable remote collaboration and meeting scheduling—enhancing the work setting for everyone in the firm.

These are just some of the ways to shift the thinking about how work is done. Indeed, a broader palette of possibilities is established when you think differently about process execution. Of course, careful attention is needed to help your people maintain their focus as they start to implement the changes you need them to make.

Maintaining Staff's Focus

With so much change afoot in the pursuit of indispensability, it is no wonder that some of your best people's attention may drift a bit. Often they need a mental break while things are being figured out. Of course, a lack of focus can slow progress, hurt execution, and dilute morale. So it's your job to keep them focused.

Try these ideas to keep your staffer's heads in the game:

1. **Help them see that they're part of something bigger than themselves.** As pointed out earlier in the book, people need to possess a sense of belonging to do their best each day. Let them know that others are counting on them to do their jobs. This will provide an extra boost to help them refocus on being part of the team.

2. **Give their work meaning by clarifying their new roles and responsibilities.** Connect the dots for them. Help them see why what they do is an essential part of the organization's becoming indispensable.

   For example, we started every change project at The Home Depot with the "why." This provided team members with needed clarity of purpose, and it helped explain how the project was intending to make a difference for the retailer.

3. **Use special assignments to get them reengaged.** Providing work variety can recharge your people. What better way to provide variety than assigning someone a role on a special project? It provides a break from their day-to-day activities and it enables the company to cover more ground.

   We used this technique quite successfully at Mitsui Sumitomo. Staff members at the insurer were thirsty for change, and being assigned a role on a vision-related project team was seen as a special honor bestowed to only a select few. Consequently, almost all of the headquarters staff wanted the opportunity to contribute.

4. **Make them better and they'll recommit.** Provide training and learning opportunities to inspire new interest in the work at hand.

This makes your workforce stronger and it gives your more ambitious staffers something new to learn.

The COVID-19 crisis enabled many businesses to provide their people with new learning opportunities. For example, consumer banks needed to increase employee cross-training in specific services as demand for mortgage-refinance applications surged. Banks also had to train employees in empathy as they helped distressed clients use digital tools and new products and services.[7]

5. **Introduce them to new people.** Provide opportunities for staffers to get in front of other employees. This can be accomplished by having them prepare and deliver briefings about the work that they're doing. It can be accomplished by inviting them to meetings where others are doing the same. It's amazing how effective this technique can be in reenergizing your team.

We used this quite often at LexisNexis. It was a way to help the software business learn about the other parts of the company. It also served to inform and enlighten colleagues who knew little about the software side of the house.

Get people involved with other staff members and watch their commitment grow.

Yes, it can be this simple. Provide your team with a sense of purpose. Make them see how what they do matters. Deliver some variety. Keep them interested in the changes you need to make on your road to indispensability.

Of course, sometimes more care is needed to ensure that they (and you) remain resilient. After all, change is *tough stuff*, and you need your people to be *tough* too.

On Remaining Resilient

Resiliency is a "must have" for every indispensable business. If the pandemic wasn't enough to convince you of the vital importance of building a resilient business, I'm not sure what will. It is what enables your staffers to get up each morning and give you their all. It helps them dust themselves off and carry on after unexpected challenges and disruptions emerge during the course of the day. Resiliency is the characteristic that you must cultivate to ensure enduring success. Without it, you will fail.

Because a resilient culture is built one person at a time, the burden is on you to ensure your people have what it takes to overcome the negative effects that everyday stressors convey. The good news is that resiliency can be taught, and you need to teach your people how to be resilient so that you can establish the kind of company culture that can withstand anything that comes its way.

An oft-forgotten but essential part of an effective change management philosophy, resiliency training is your best defense against the malaise that can cripple an organization that lacks resilience.

There are four facets to resiliency. They comprise the mental, physical, social, and spiritual aspects of each person.

- The **mental** aspects have to do with one's ability to self-regulate their reactions to stressors. Resiliency training should include assisting people in reframing thoughts, managing change, and raising one's self-awareness so they can master self-regulation.
- The **physical** aspects have to do with one's habits. Resiliency training should include tips for getting proper sleep, good nutrition, and exercise.
- The **social** aspects have to do with one's relationship management. Resiliency training should include ideas for improving one's connectedness with others.
- The **spiritual** aspects have to do with one's core values. Resiliency training should include an exploration of one's guiding principles and purpose.

Your goal should be to establish a community of resilient leaders who can serve as role models and mentors to everyone in the organization.

Many companies are already taking action to build a resilient culture. Johnson & Johnson, for example, promotes resiliency through its Human Performance Institute's Corporate Athlete Resilience Program. According to the company, "Corporate Athlete Resilience takes a holistic, science-based approach to sustainable behavior change, enabling people to understand different types of stress, recognize how to best respond to stress productively, and learn how to train to build resilience every day so they can recover, adapt and grow from stress."[8]

You've got to make a similar commitment to building a program that can make your people resilient too.

Here's a simple way to get your program started:

1. **Build it:** Many training firms offer canned packages that you can use. I prefer to cocreate my resiliency programs with client staffers. They know what the current culture is like, and working with them enables me to use exactly the right ingredients to make resiliency stick for the client.

2. **Pilot it:** Once the program is built, deliver it. See how your people respond. Do they feel that they've learned some coping techniques? Are there weak spots in the training that need tightening up? Use the feedback to improve the training content.

3. **Reinforce it:** Coaching helps the training stick. My program includes ongoing coaching because I know that resiliency techniques require practice and reinforcement in order to become part of one's stress management repertoire.

4. **Measure it:** Track how your people are doing in the face of adversity. Are your people holding strong? Absenteeism, productivity, and employee retention measurement are all valid metrics to use when determining the effectiveness of your resiliency training. If those aren't tracking positively, your training approach may not be working.

Remember, when you change behavior, you change the culture. By folding resiliency training into your employee offerings, you begin to shape-shift the way staffers behave. Their beliefs, expectations, attitudes, and conduct will change for the better the more resilient they become.

Of course, leadership is needed to compel and motivate others to change the way they approach their work as well. Give some thought to how you intend to provide the kind of compelling leadership necessary to inspire continuous change.

Compelling Leadership

Being indispensable begins with a dream. Think Bezos, Jobs, and Musk. They all possessed a vision that helped them build great companies. We can argue that each is quite compelling in his own way. You need to be compelling in your own way too.

Here are a few ways that leaders who may not be on everyone's radar screen are providing their own brand of compelling leadership. My hope is that their examples inspire you to develop your own approach of inspiring others to follow you.

Doug Conant wrote notes. As Campbell Soup's CEO, Doug Conant sent employees more than thirty thousand handwritten notes recognizing their successes and contributions to achieving the vision.[9] People at the soup company would hang these notes in their cubicles and offices. They were cherished because they were handwritten.

Taking the time to say thank you in a heartfelt way (and what is more heartfelt than a handwritten note?) does wonders in promoting followership.

Ron Harder told stories. People love stories. They're how we learn. They're the way in which customs and traditions are passed on from one generation to the next. A story gives us a method that enables deeper understanding.

Ron Harder, former president of Jeweler's Mutual, used storytelling as a means to reinforce the behaviors among his staff that he knew were needed to make the specialty insurer vital in a time of great consolidation in his industry. He regularly started company town hall meetings with stories about growing up a farmer's son and the values that his tough upbringing instilled in him from an early age—the ethics of working hard, playing fair, and giving credit were often highlighted. His *down-home* approach to storytelling resonated with his people.

Sharing stories and anecdotes can help make you more compelling.

Koji Yoshida struck up conversations. The former president of Mitsui Sumitomo's U.S. operations would often walk the halls of the company and strike up conversations with random staff members about the company's vision and the transformation that he was leading. As the word got out that Yoshida was doing this sort of thing, staffers quickly learned that they needed to keep up with their company's progress and get involved in the change effort.

These short conversations can go a long way toward promoting engagement and inspiring unity among personnel. So don't just stand there! Start walking around and strike up conversations that show you care about the changes that you're promoting.

Gary Whited celebrated vision-inspired behavior. Prior to his retirement, hardly a day went by that Gary Whited, then president of GDLS, didn't bring up an example of someone in the company doing something in support of the company's vision. He would do it at staff meetings, project status reviews, customer visits—he called out the positive things that people were doing to make GDLS a better company.

By distinguishing and applauding vision-inspired behavior, Whited was demonstrating his commitment to the transformative work we were doing at the company, and he was encouraging others to follow suit. We can all do the same by recognizing others' contributions to the cause.

Indeed, compelling leadership is about connecting with your people. It takes thoughtful effort, and that effort pays dividends as your organization becomes more indispensable in the marketplace. Infinite possibilities open up when a leader can compel others to follow.

Strive to be compelling and you can make good things happen too.

Some Final Thoughts on Change Management

Japanese author Haruki Murakami once wrote, "Pain is inevitable, suffering is optional."

While the path to indispensability is momentously challenging, your staff members need not suffer. Rather, your change efforts can be the source of inspiration and freedom—the idea of your business never failing is an attractive one, after all. The difference, as Murakami suggests, is one's attitude. You and your people have the choice to see change as either misery or opportunity.

As the chapter comes to a close, consider these eight features of solid change management:

1. **Leadership behavior:** Your leadership behavior must properly align with your vision for indispensability. Misalignment leads to widespread doubt as staff members begin to wonder if you're truly committed to making the changes that you espouse.

   Elon Musk, for example, is said to routinely work eighty-hour workweeks at Tesla. Staffers there know that he is committed to the notion of making the automaker indispensable.

   Be sure to walk the talk or no one will follow.

2. **Strategy rollout:** People need to know the plan, so be transparent and communicate it.

   When JPMorgan Chase decided to go digital, for example, it initially used a series of town hall meetings across the country to help broadcast its consumer banking strategy, called "Mobile First, Digital Everything." The idea, driven by chairman and CEO Jamie Dimon, is to help all JPM staff understand the move into the digital age and not leave anyone behind as the bank continues to invest in the changes needed to become "the easiest bank to do business with."[10]

   Be sure that your staff can comprehend and understand what their role is in helping you execute the strategies and achieve the intent.

3. **Communication conventions:** As in the last chapter, communication vacuums will often be filled with misinformation. Get ahead of that by using multiple communication channels to deliver your messaging to all staffers before someone fills the void with speculation and conjecture.

GDLS used its intranet, newsletters, and "lunch 'n' learn" meetings as a means to broadcast its project status reports, for example. It is a wonderful way to ensure people have ample opportunity to understand what's going on.

4. **Brand promise:** Your brand must deliver what it promises to deliver. If you pride yourself on competing on price, be sure you are the low-cost producer in your industry. If you compete on service, be sure you deliver an outstanding customer experience all the time.

   JPM's company values, for example, focus on exceptional client service, operational excellence, and a commitment to integrity, fairness, and responsibility.[11] As the largest bank in the United States, JPM has built a winning culture that is fully aligned with what a bank that wants to become "the easiest bank to do business with" should be.

5. **Technology assimilation:** Indispensability requires technology. Why? Because people use technology to do everything! If you don't leverage technology in the delivery of your product or service, you just won't become indispensable.

   Clearly, the leadership team at Spirit AeroSystems, a leading manufacturer of aircraft fuselages, wants to make their company indispensable. They use technology. The company is in the midst of a major overhaul in its technology infrastructure as it works to institutionalize advanced model-based engineering and supply-chain management practices as part of its transformation effort, for example.[12]

6. **Organizational construct:** Your organizational design has to match your culture. Yes, you will need to invest in training and people because the best constructs require ample empowerment of frontline staff. But that investment will pay dividends.

   Zappos serves as a great example of a company that has done a fine job in aligning its organizational design with its culture. It employs a flatter, self-managed/self-organized design because, as explained on its website:

Zappos has always been focused on delivering exceptional customer service—we call it WOW service. To provide WOW service, it's important that every employee understands our customers' needs, and has the ability to improve the customer experience whenever possible. As our company grew, we became slower to sense and respond to customer feedback, because of the layers employees needed to go through to get things done. Holacracy (i.e., a predefined set of rules and processes, checks and balances, and guidelines that an organization can use to help them become self-managed) is a tool that allows every employee to quickly surface and act on customer feedback, so we can continuously provide WOW service, regardless of the size of our company.

The alignment of organizational design and reporting structures with company culture is an essential ingredient for indispensability.

7. **Staff readiness:** You have to be sure that your people are ready to deliver. It is a nonnegotiable aspect of being indispensable.

For instance, the majority of Zappos' staff attends regularly scheduled training sessions to ensure that everyone there is on the same page about current policies and procedures. This strengthens how self-management is achieved. It reinforces the values that are most important at Zappos.

8. **Measurement and reward alignment:** Measure for outcomes and desired behavior will follow.

For example, Tesla has set aggressive growth goals as part of its transformation strategy—targeting the production of five thousand Model 3 cars every week. Consequently, it must run its production "lean 'n' mean." It's no wonder that it has adopted a rank and yank performance management approach—one that rewards top performers with compensation, equity awards, and promotions and shows low performers the door.[13]

Aligning measurements and rewards is working at Tesla, and it will work for you.

To Close

Indeed, change is inevitable. How you drive and manage it is up to you. My hope is that you choose to *test-drive* some of the concepts provided here. I know, through my experience in developing these ideas with my clients, that they will deliver results. You just need to try them. When you do, you'll see for yourself just how essential a solid change management approach is when pursuing indispensability.

In our last chapter, we will explore some additional ideas and concepts about how to build an enduring business that your customers can't live without. It's about how to ensure lasting indispensability.

Chapter 7's Indispensable Top Ten List

These ten takeaways will help you make the changes needed within your business so it can become indispensable. Be sure to take a deeper dive into other key concepts by reviewing the chapter in detail.

1. The vast majority of organizations require "big changes" if they want to become indispensable. Big changes require a good deal of time. Consequently, proper preparation is required.
2. Demonstrate "true" executive sponsorship for the effort by identifying yourself as the sponsor of the change program.
3. Push for stickiness as you go about revitalizing your business and you'll begin to see ways to become indispensable.
4. The bifurcation of responsibilities creates a "silo effect" that serves to separate, rather than integrate, the core functions that comprise a business.
5. As your transformation to indispensability evolves and moves through the organization, it is important to replace command and control thinking with the notion of "boundaryless" process flow.
6. Artificial job role boundaries and established ways of doing work often impede exceptional performance and inhibit businesses from becoming indispensable.

7. You can begin to build a better mousetrap, one that can make you indispensable, when you begin to think differently about how work is performed.

8. Resiliency must be woven into the DNA of an indispensable business. It enables the company to better anticipate, prepare for, respond to, and adapt to ever-increasing market disruptions, shifts in customer preferences, and challenging competitor tactics that can knock a business off its hinges.

9. Exceptional leadership is needed to compel and motivate others to change. Give some thought to how you intend to provide the kind of compelling leadership necessary to inspire the changes needed to become indispensable.

10. While the path to indispensability is momentously challenging, your staff members need not suffer. Rather, your change efforts can be the source of inspiration and freedom. It's up to you to make them so.

How to Ensure Lasting Indispensability

BY NOW, YOU'VE COME TO realize that lasting indispensability takes work—and lots of it!

It is no easy job to make a customer for life. It requires attention to the details and striving to follow the Indispensability Agenda outlined in this book, including establishing the "right" traits:

- vision
- leadership
- culture
- people
- trust and empowerment
- change frameworks

However, there is a whole slew of other, subtler elements to ensure enduring indispensability. This chapter is intended to bring to light some of the finer points that should be added to the fundamental framework provided in earlier chapters. Consider the ideas presented in this, our final chapter, as the "spices" that will forever make your company completely irresistible in the markets that you serve.

Adding Spices to the Mix

Trust has been emphasized throughout the book. It's a key factor in forging relationships that last a lifetime. Clearly, it must be part of an indispensable company's DNA. Trust drives mutual respect among staff, and it leads to that feeling of being "in it together," which is also essential to consistently delivering an exceptional customer experience.

Indeed, top leadership sets the tone here by behaving in ways that demonstrate their willingness to protect, defend, and serve their people. It's the combination of trust and leadership skills that builds the culture needed to become indispensable among your customers.

We'll expand the thinking in this chapter by exploring these six finer points of indispensable culture-building:

1. Don't overmanage.
2. Ensure your team of leaders "fit" the mold.
3. Develop Next-Gen leaders for future indispensability.
4. Think through your ecosystems.
5. Jettison the wrong kinds of customers.
6. Avoid the seven deadly sins of change.

Let's take a deeper dive into each of these aspects of ensuring lasting indispensability.

Don't Overmanage

It's part of the human condition to want to do a great job. Consequently, some leaders fall prone to overmanaging their organizations. This only hurts your chance of ever becoming indispensable in the marketplace. This can manifest itself in several ways, including the following.

Hero disease. Like it or not, as a top leader, you are setting the bar for others to clear. There's no need for you to steal the show from your team. Let them shine. It lowers burnout, both yours and theirs, and makes your job a whole lot easier because you have an entire team sharing the workload.

Hero disease, and the burnout that comes with it, is something that deserves your attention. In fact, a Harvard Business School study estimates that stress-related burnout may inflict a health-care cost of $125 to $190 billion a year in the United States alone.[1]

So before you bring disaster to your organization through your overzealous, heroic behavior, create an atmosphere where your strongest staffers can perform—enabling them to help you bring about indispensability.

Lack of patience. Change takes time. After all, you're asking people to learn new behaviors and put them into use. Leaders must maintain their dedication to the cause for as long as it takes to achieve the changes envisioned.

All of the leaders highlighted in the book, including Jobs and Welch, Dimon and Musk, Deep and Bezos, have had to weather storms and overcome obstacles to build companies worthy of becoming indispensable.

Too often, cultural transformation efforts are canceled before they are given the time needed to take hold. Don't let your eagerness to overmanage sabotage your pursuit of indispensability.

Constant restructuring. Too much top leadership shuffling creates instability within an organization. Instability prohibits indispensability.

Former BMW chief executive Harald Krüger, for example, forged a reputation for relentless leadership team shuffling.[2] None of it proved to deliver much financial benefit to the company in the four years that he was at the helm. As a result, he was replaced by Oliver Zipse in August 2019. Krüger was just another casualty of overmanagement.

It is impossible to convince staffers that everything is running smoothly if you're regularly turning over your C-suite. Instead, work to surround yourself with great people and embolden them to work as one.

Solo artistry. Want to make your staffers feel belittled and slighted? Go it alone. Don't include them in setting direction or managing change. Many who overmanage develop a belief that they need to do everything themselves in order to *get it right*. However, your *solo artistry* is a surefire way to limit your business to being second-rate, at best.

Take the case of Adam Neumann, cofounder of WeWork, the commercial real estate company that provides shared workspaces, who had to step down from his CEO post because, in the words of one WeWork staffer, "Nothing could happen without Adam."[3]

Rather than feeling the need to run the entire show, create occasions to join forces by seeking opportunities, in groups and one-on-one sessions, to solicit and gain your team's viewpoints and ideas for problem-solving. This creates the strength in numbers needed to become indispensable.

Micromanaging. Smothering your people is another sign of overmanagement. Please realize that an incessant need to control every action and orchestrate every moment is hurting your team's performance.

Steve Jobs is an example of an executive who had to learn this lesson the hard way. His first stint at Apple didn't end well, and he struggled with micromanagement at NeXT Computer, too, as exemplified in a *New York Times* article, where it was reported that "Mr. Jobs spent 20 minutes directing the landscaping crew on the exact placement of the sprinkler heads."[4]

Fortunately, by the time he returned to Apple, he got better at empowering the people around him, including his eventual successor, Tim Cook.

A good team needs space to perform at their best. Learn to trust them and they will begin to trust you!

Thirst for profits. Many overmanage out of a thirst for profits. They think that they can squeeze every dime out of their business by pushing their people nonstop. If profits are the only thing driving your behavior, you will be unable to build an indispensable business. Simply, your greed will get in the way.

Consider what's happened with the Sackler family business, Purdue Pharma. Lawsuits allege the company and the Sackler family are responsible for starting and sustaining the opioid crisis in the United States. It seems that greed has led to their demise. The maker of OxyContin filed for Chapter 11 in September 2019, as the company continues to struggle to settle the more than two thousand lawsuits brought against it.

You don't want to let greed stand between your business and its indispensability.

Indeed, most of these behaviors and tendencies listed here are a result of unchecked selfishness and/or a dangerous lack of self-confidence. Great leaders do not overmanage. Instead, they work at exhibiting the behaviors that promote trust, fair play, and teamwork. Be that kind of leader.

Ensure Your Team of Leaders "Fit" the Mold

By this point in the book, you recognize a direct correlation between indispensability and the leaders who oversee the company. As discussed throughout, you must put the "right" players in place and enable them for success. Your team of leaders is no exception.

All of them must inspire others to perform at their best. Therefore, you need leaders who fit the mold for driving indispensable behaviors within your company.

Here are ten key assessment questions[5] to consider when evaluating your current team of leaders (and those who aspire to join the team in the future, regardless of whether these candidates come from within or outside of the organization):

1. **Does the leader work to understand their industry and contribute to its evolution through their company's work?** You want leaders who are sincerely interested in the work at hand and those who can become movers and shakers within their industries.

   BMW's recently named CEO Oliver Zipse is an example of a leader who rose through the ranks via industry expertise. As *Automotive News* reported, "Zipse is known as a factory strategist. . . . He has a zeal for the intricacies of flexible manufacturing—something the company must master to juggle development and production of electric and internal combustion vehicles."[6]

Cultivated from within, the twenty-eight-year BMW veteran offers the right "fit" for where the German automaker must go next.

Cultivating leaders who can offer deep industry know-how can make a company indispensable.

2. **Does the leader communicate the firm's vision and strategies and help their team better understand how they contribute to the achievement of company goals?** You want leaders who understand, buy into, and can communicate the firm's strategies to their people.

3. **Is the leader an exceptional trust-builder?** You want leaders of high integrity who can be counted on.

   Former Microsoft CEO Steve Ballmer is famous for saying, "I always reserve the right to get smarter."[7]

   Humble leadership instills trust and confidence within an indispensable business. Trust-building is a characteristic that should be forged into your team of leaders.

4. **Does the leader demonstrate executive presence and inspire confidence at all levels of an organization?** You want leaders who have the poise and sure-handedness to be effective in all circumstances.

5. **Does the leader inspire followership and have the ability to build a strong team around them?** You want leaders who people want to work for and with.

   Former CEO of The Home Depot, Frank Blake, saw the value of "getting in the trenches." Blake would often travel to Home Depot stores, put on the orange apron, and join staff on the frontlines.[8]

   It's this type of leader who you're looking to grow within your business.

6. **Is the leader an outstanding communicator, skilled at both listening and messaging?** You want leaders who can communicate effectively so that there is no doubt about what is important.

   Regardless of your politics, Gov. Cuomo was widely recognized, at the onset of the pandemic, as a powerful communicator who provided needed empathy, transparency, encouragement, and accountability. His outstanding aptitude for keeping his communications simple and to the point was largely credited with getting New Yorkers to modify their behaviors last year in the best interests of public health.

Cuomo's performance throughout the crisis serves as a superb example of the power of communicating well.

7. **Is the leader a "thought leader" who can introduce new ways of "thinking" and "doing"?** You want leaders who are always pushing to be better.

   Many of the leaders discussed in the book exemplify this quality. For inspiration, think Bezos, Jobs, and Musk.

   People who think outside the box can provide a nice complement to any leadership team.

8. **Does the leader reward outstanding performance and know how to reward the "right" people?** You want leaders who recognize talent and reward people based on results, not based on effort or out of favoritism.

9. **Does the leader routinely provide feedback and coaching to their team?** You want leaders who are always working to make their teams better.

   Garry Ridge, CEO of WD-40 Company, is a leader who operates under this principle. In his 2009 book, *Helping People Win at Work*,[9] coauthored with Ken Blanchard, Ridge suggests that coaching, development, and feedback should be an everyday conversation between leader and direct report. His company enjoys employee engagement numbers in excess of 90 percent.[10]

   Look for this leadership trait in your team.

10. **Can the leader demystify complex concepts and teach them to their teams?** You want leaders who can teach people how to be the best that they can be.

Certainly, these ten questions are essential in the assessment of leaders. However, they are not intended to represent the full suite of questions needed to do a thorough evaluation. In fact, many of my clients choose to use them to design a rubric that properly weighs each assessment question so to better address their particular situation. For instance, a company addressing trust issues may weigh trust-related questions higher than ones related to, perhaps, rewarding performance or new ways of thinking. The weighing enables them to objectively establish a relative "leadership fit" score that matters to them.

Additionally, please note that a hiring manager / hiring committee can leverage these kinds of questions in a variety of ways, including within a 360 evaluation process, by management team survey, or simply by using it as an interview script. These questions can also provide value when considering promoting Next-Gen leaders to management positions—proper "fit" is an important consideration when choosing future leaders for your company.

Develop Next-Gen Leaders for Future Indispensability

You have to be deliberate in developing your next generation of leaders. It doesn't just happen. Done right, it makes your path to indispensability much smoother because you will have cultivated a whole generation of dependable leaders behind you. These people will be the ones who lead the continuous evolution of your business for years to come.

Of course, you have to position these Next-Gen leaders in places where they can both learn and have an immediate impact. After all, their leadership style and behaviors will shape-shift the culture of your business as they inherit the helm. Your investment in the *right* young leaders today will pay dividends in years to come.

Here are six tips to help you identify and grow your Next-Gen leader talent:

1. **Be a talent scout.** Always be on the lookout for talent, wherever it resides. Dig deep to identify those people worth developing—ones who can, one day, earn a spot on your team of leaders.

   As mentioned in chapter 5, I recommend the establishment of a Gen Y committee as a means to spot and develop talent. We used the technique at The Hartford with good results.

Every year, a dozen high-potential staffers (as designated by their managers) were identified and given an assignment to tackle one of the claims division's operating challenges. They would meet quarterly with Paul Schwartzott, EVP of claims (now retired), over the course of the year and report on their progress and receive feedback and coaching. At year-end, the team presented their recommendations to Schwartzott and his leadership team.

The committee membership would change every year, and each reconstituted committee would tackle a different problem. For example, one year the committee examined the loss report assignment challenge; another year it went after improving reserve accuracy. Regardless, it proved to be a terrific way for younger employees to gain top leader exposure while working on improving the claim-handling function at the insurer. It also helped Schwartzott and his senior leaders gain insight into the potential of some of their younger staffers.

2. **Coach them up.** The best way to prepare young talent is to provide them solid coaching—the kind that enables them to learn from other strong leaders.

Within my coaching practice, I get the opportunity to coach many high-potential Next-Gen people. Most are eager to learn, and all appreciate having someone with whom to rehearse and practice. Examining recent work situations, ones that were particularly stressful or offered no clear resolution, has proven to be quite effective in helping younger people glean additional insight and explore other options for use the next time they find themselves facing a similar set of circumstances.

Create an environment where Next-Gen staffers have access to the coaching they need to reach their full potential.

3. **Don't be prescriptive.** If you want your leaders to develop into ones you can count on and trust, don't define every action for them to take. Instead, be sure to make your intent clear and let them determine how to get it done. Just be sure to let them know that you're available should they need your support or counsel.

Chris Brown, VP of the MENA Market at GDLS, is a master at this kind of leadership. A retired Canadian army officer, Brown is a top leader who understands the need to develop talent. His approach includes "coaching up" his team and letting them do their thing. His open-door policy keeps his calendar packed. However, he has cultivated many future leaders for the defense company.

This is a great way to build a squad of empowered young leaders.

4. **Be deliberate with decision authority.** Not every leader has the *right* to make every decision. Be sure your Next-Gen leaders understand which decisions are theirs to make and which need escalation.

Dave Crocker, VP of Engineering at GDLS, involves his people in setting their decision rights, mutually agreeing to the conditions in when his leaders can act independently—and which situations require them to involve him in direction-setting.

Crocker's approach to decision rights is a fine way to engage a team and ensure their understanding and buy-in to their decision-making authority.

5. **Redirect wisely.** Keeping in mind that Next-Gen staffers are still developing their *leadership chops*, it's important not to be quick to veto their ideas and approaches. Instead, provide the space for them to learn while doing. Sure, you want to remain close enough to the action to know when to intervene. But you also want to create learning moments for them to garner valuable lessons in leadership too.

The Hartford's Schwartzott did a noble job applying this principle with his Gen Y committee. He was careful not to rip into his young staffers at the quarterly reviews. Instead, he established a coaching environment and used the time to gently guide and direct the team.

6. **Maintain the focus on outcomes.** As already mentioned, be sure to make your expectations clear and hold your people to them. You want to be sure that they do things the right way, the first time. Don't tolerate less than total commitment to being indispensable.

VP Don Kotchman heads the U.S. Market at GDLS. If his team falls short of his expectations, Kotchman routinely reminds them that customers surely won't accept anything less than their best efforts and neither should any of them. By fixating on achievement, Kotchman makes his leaders tougher and better prepared for tomorrow's challenges.

These are just some of the ways that you can prepare your Next-Gen leaders to earn a place on your leadership team. The centerpiece of all of these ideas is dependability. You need to build leaders who are dependable in order to become indispensable.

Dependability is an essential element of maintaining a company's place within its greater ecosystem as well.

Think through Your Ecosystems

Like it or not, your business is part of a bigger, more comprehensive ecosystem. Your business is not an island unto itself. For example, you may rely on suppliers, wholesalers, installers, and the like to get your business to hum. Similarly, you may be a business that provides the same to other businesses. Business-to-business (B2B) relationships can be challenging due to service, pricing, delivery schedules, and multi-channel sales problems.

Here are some ways that you can improve your B2B relationships and enhance your standing within your ecosystem:

1. **Know yourself.** You simply can't be *all* things to *all* people. Understand your brand promise. Do you compete on price? Is it feature-rich products that set your business apart from all the rest? You have to know yourself and your value proposition to appropriately expand your ecosystem.

   An operating unit of the Nestlé Group, Nespresso produces and sells premium-priced single-serve coffee and espresso capsules. It differentiates itself from other single-serve coffee products on quality. Its rich, creamy taste—not the machines used to brew its coffee pods—separates Nespresso coffee from its competitors.

That said, Nespresso needed to extend its ecosystem to include coffee machine manufacturers willing to produce Nespresso-compatible machines[11] in order to launch worldwide. By doing so, Nespresso was able to jump into the market without having to absorb the cost of coffee machine manufacturing. Yet because its capsules and brewing method are patented, Nespresso was able to keep competitors from easily entering the market.

It is a wonderful example of a company that expanded market share by sticking to the things that make it stand out among its competition while cultivating needed B2B partners to make it work.

2. **Discover mutual benefits.** What can your business bring to the table to complement your partner's capabilities? Are there ways to team together to get more things done? Can you offer preferred pricing or deliver customized product sets that solve some your partner's greatest business challenges? Seek synergies and expand your ecosystem.

With an eye to extending its ecosystem, Nespresso helped its B2B partners, including Krups, Breville, and DeLonghi, expand their markets too. These companies produce the machines that make the Nespresso coffee.

3. **Look to "scale" all that you do.** Flawless business execution builds market share. Look to scale your operations to best match your B2B partner's operating models. You can make your business indispensable to partners by shifting operations and workforce to meet their changing demands.

Recent research conducted by SAP and Oxford Economics supports the point about the importance of enabling workforce scalability. They surveyed eight hundred senior executives in sixteen industries from fourteen countries and found the following:[12]

- 44 percent of workforce spend is on the external workforce.
- 65 percent of respondents report that their external workforce is important or essential to operating at full capacity and meeting market demands.

- 62 percent of respondents say their external workforce enables them to improve the company's overall financial performance.
- 68 percent of respondents report that they need external workers to help develop and improve their products and services.

Clearly, *scalability* is not only needed to handle business dips and meet demand during high growth cycles but is an important part of a company's growth and profitability equation.

4. **Find ecosystem partners with integrative technology.** There are all kinds of dependable cloud-based computing and data analytics capabilities available in the marketplace. Look for business partners who are open to bridging the digital divide. These businesses are more likely to possess the technological capabilities to quickly enable business integration.

Apple's open platform HealthKit is an example of this idea in action. It offers the potential to establish an ecosystem of physicians, researchers, hospitals, patients, and developers of health-care and fitness apps that can offer customers an entirely unique set of products and services that may not be available except through HealthKit.

Integrative technologies help forge essential integration points that expand your reach and influence within your ecosystem. Be sure to consider this when charting your path to indispensability.

5. **Fold trust into the equation.** Full transparency among your ecosystem partners eliminates surprises and fosters a deepening of your business relationships. Of course, integrated systems can help. However, *real* trust is built by delivering on promises. Do this and watch how mutual business interests grow and mature within your ecosystem.

Consider the teamwork taking place between BMW and Daimler. Once fierce rivals, the two luxury car manufacturers announced that they are investing $1.13 billion in joint ride- and car-sharing as well as electric vehicle charging projects.

As reported by CNBC, the new program will focus on five areas:[13]

a. *Free Now*, an Uber-style ride-sharing service;
b. *Share Now*, which will replace and expand Car2Go's car-sharing operations;
c. *Charge Now*, an electric vehicle charging network;
d. *Park Now*, a service that will help motorists not just find available parking but even book a space ahead of time; and
e. *Reach Now*, a smartphone-based route management and transportation service.

It is an interesting alliance—one that signifies the way ecosystem players (even competitors) can leverage and reshape relationships to competitive gain.

Indeed, B2B partnering can provide needed support as you pursue your Indispensability Agenda. Just don't underestimate the work required to leverage these tips. Be ready to do whatever it takes to be exceptional in all that you do.

Sometimes this work may even require jettisoning a customer or partner.

Jettisoning the Wrong Kinds of Stakeholders

Often considered unthinkable, dumping the wrong kinds of customers or partners is an essential part of becoming indispensable.

Some clients may never be satisfied. Some partners may be undependable or unreasonable. If this happens, it can negatively influence your ability to keep your promises to other customers and business partners. It's then that you must jettison this toxic business relationship.

Here are a few examples from an oft-quoted *Harvard Business Review* article on the subject:[14]

- Sprint jettisoned customers who were frequently calling into its customer support line.
- AT&T did it to its consumer internet customers when it decided to focus on its commercial customers instead.

- Allstate and Nationwide did it to customers living in hurricane areas.
- The University of Texas Medical Branch in Galveston did it to deadbeat patients by requiring them to pay up-front for service.
- Marsh & McLennan did it to customers who were deemed nonprofitable.

Before you begin to take action, though, be sure to consider these unintended consequences and account for how you will manage them as you jettison problematic stakeholders:[15]

1. **Brand reputation:** Clearly, there is a risk that your brand will suffer in the marketplace when firing a customer or partner. To manage this risk, it's essential that you be deliberate in handling the spin—both inside and out. Internally, communicating clearly on the reasons that led to the decision to flush business relations should be discussed with key leaders. Your people should come to understand why the move was important to the business. Messaging outside is a bit trickier. You must be delicate in the way that the information is shared because you absolutely cannot damage the reputation of a former customer or former partner.

2. **Revenue impact:** When firing a customer, it's important to compare the revenue lost to the costs in keeping the customer. Depending on the circumstances, the calculation may actually prove to provide a gain on the play. But when it doesn't, time must be taken to offset revenue projections and recalibrate related internal measurement / commission structures to keep any affected personnel whole. You don't want your sales team, for example, to feel the pain of a lost customer.

3. **Morale:** Morale could likely tick upward when word gets out that you've fired a particularly tough customer or business partner. But keep an eye on that because you don't want a negative reaction to ripple through your business and affect behavior down the line.

4. **Service delivery changes:** Modifying how service is delivered going forward is an important idea to keep top of mind whenever firing a customer. An overhaul of your service delivery model can be needed to prevent this kind of negative customer relationship from coming up again in the future. The same is true in severing an ecosystem partner relationship.

5. **Redefining customer targets:** Another important consideration is related to your customer and partner profiles. If you don't have these, then you may want to create ones that can be used to qualify customer and partner targets. If these do exist, they may need refinement and adjustment to ensure that ideal customers and partners are being pursued and less desirable customers and partners are not being chased. Proper targeting can be helpful in avoiding future business relationship problems.

This list represents only a handful of the considerations to ponder when determining the need to end a difficult business relationship. However, these five things are important to contemplate as you begin to jettison nerve-rattling customers and business partners.

As we wind down our discussion on becoming indispensable, let's take a moment to look at some of the things that should absolutely be avoided at all costs in your pursuit of being a company that your customers can't live without. Think of them as the Seven Deadly Sins of Indispensable Change.

The Seven Deadly Sins of Indispensable Change

It has taken nearly thirty years of working with some of the best organizations on the planet for me to know that a business will spoil any chance of becoming indispensable should it fall prey to any of these Seven Deadly Sins of indispensable change:

1. **No vision:** People need a reason to believe. Give them one. Craft a vision story so compelling that your staffers can't help but become captivated by the possibilities that it presents. Drive that vision

story deep into the fabric of the business by deliberately translating the details into action. Demonstrate through your behavior the kind of business you want to command.

Be sure to use assorted delivery devices to promote the vision story because people learn in many different ways. You'll recall these examples from earlier in the book:

- LexisNexis developed a Customized Vision Magazine that presented the tank builder's vision story through a series of related articles.
- Jewelers Mutual sponsored an internal vision trade show, where its management team delivered the vision story to staffers through a series of briefings presented at presentation booths that personnel visited as they gathered the various promotional giveaways available at each one.
- The Hartford crafted vision storyboards to present the vision through a series of visual representations similar to a comic strip. Later, these storyboards were distributed as desk mats to staff members for easy reference.

Be sure to articulate your vision and communicate it to your people.

2. **No plan:** Of course, you need a plan for achieving your vision for indispensability. Build one. Be sure it includes the definition of the various initiatives required to move the organization from where it is to where it needs to be.

   Further, be sure not to *kid* yourself into thinking that your budget is a plan. It's not. I cannot begin to tell you how many times I've visited prospective clients, ones who *swear up and down* that they have a robust strategic plan, only to discover their budget is what they mean. Budgeting is not strategic planning!

   To reiterate, you will not achieve your vision for indispensability without having a plan to get there—construct one and follow it.

3. **No discipline:** Indispensability requires great focus and discipline. Without these, it's easy to get distracted—the business world hurls too many challenges at you every day to remain diligent—if

discipline is lacking. Therefore, it's wise to organize change efforts into separate initiatives that can be managed with great rigor.

It's for this reason, for example, that Steve Franz, long-time GDLS VP, was recently assigned the task to put in place an orderly and repeatable process for executing customer programs.

You can't just throw things against the wall and hope that they stick. Discipline is necessary to sustain the level of transformation to make your business indispensable.

4. **No executive sponsorship:** Your executive team must *own* the work at hand. They do that by sponsoring change initiatives and knocking out any obstacles that project teams confront along the way.

   Consider the many examples discussed in the book, from GDLS' policy requiring VP-level executive sponsorship on every change effort to Skillshare's CEO Michael Karnjanaprakorn's willingness to solicit input from staffers on key decisions. Executive participation in business transformation is an *absolute must*.

   Remember, if you fail to demonstrate your commitment through active participation, your people will begin to lose interest in your change effort too.

5. **No communication:** Change is intimidating, and it's only natural for staffers to resist it. Be sure that you're properly communicating both intent and progress through a variety of communication mechanisms. It's the only way to keep your people engaged with, and informed about, your change efforts.

   Many of the ideas for doing this are described in the book. For inspiration, recall Zappos' handwritten customer service blackboard and Jewelers Mutual's employee trade show held in an aircraft hangar. The more communication devices that you can put into place, the better.

6. **No bench strength:** Be sure to develop multiple levels of talent within your organization. Don't always press the "easy button" when choosing your special project teams. Sure, the usual suspects can be counted on (and that's why they're often selected for special

assignments). However, your other staffers are being neglected as a result. You're not providing them with the same opportunities to learn and grow.

Harken back to the example offered by LexisNexis earlier in the book, the firm instituted a rule that prohibited the use of the same personnel on every *vision-related* project. This practice spread growth opportunities among staffers and encouraged greater buy-in among personnel.

Dig deeper into our talent pool and you will harvest what's needed to maintain your path to indispensability.

7. **No ethical boundaries:** Sometimes leaders feel compelled to *stretch the truth* when business shortcomings are uncovered. This behavior is demoralizing to your people. It will "kill" all hope of good morale going forward.

There are any number of recent scandals, including price gouging at Mylan, fake account generation at Wells Fargo, emissions test cheating at Volkswagen, and slipshod data protection at Uber and Equifax, that serve as cases in point. There's no need to push ethical boundaries.

Rather than looking for ways to mislead, practice inspiring your team to do their best. By doing so, you will drive indispensability through their innovative thinking and thirst for achievement.

Indisputably, these seven deadly sins must be avoided. They will squelch any hope that you have of building an indispensable business. Of course, the good news is this: *you can avoid them by applying the ideas presented throughout the book.*

To Close

Before we bid a sweet adieu, let me offer one more bit of advice: **never settle for "good enough!"**

Simply put, "good enough" does not make it "right." In fact, putting the "right" stuff in place is at the heart of the Indispensable Agenda that I shared with you throughout this book.

To be sure, the leader of an indispensable business knows that their best work is always ahead of them. They're never satisfied with maintaining the status quo. They're always striving for more and expecting great things from themselves and their staffers alike. This is what an indispensable business is all about—never settling for second best.

That said, demonstrate your commitment to excellence by how you behave. Set the example so that your staffers understand what is expected of them too. Regularly ask yourself and your team these kinds of essential questions: *How can we do more? Improve our outcomes? Become the one that customers prefer?*

The answers to these may surprise you. The answers to these may hold the keys to indispensability.

Lastly, be sure to occasionally ask yourself, "What's next?" This is the question that will keep you in the game. It will push you to resist the urge to rest on your laurels.

Remember, the pursuit of indispensability is a marathon. It is not a sprint. You won't get there overnight. It will require focus and planning. However, it is achievable. By keeping a steady foot on the accelerator and maintaining the "right" level of intensity, you will build the kind of customer relationships that last a lifetime. You will build the kind of business that we can call *indispensable*.

Chapter 8's Indispensable Top Ten List

These ten takeaways highlight our final chapter. Be sure to take a deeper dive into other key concepts by reviewing the chapter in detail.

1. Trust has been emphasized throughout the book. It's a key factor in forging relationships that last a lifetime.
2. It's part of the human condition to want to do a great job. Consequently, some leaders fall prone to overmanaging their organizations.
3. As discussed throughout, you must put the "right" players in place and enable them for success. Your team of leaders is no exception.

4. You have to be deliberate in developing your next generation of leaders. It doesn't just happen on its own.

5. Like it or not, your business is part of a bigger, more comprehensive ecosystem.

6. B2B relationships can be challenging due to service, pricing, delivery schedules, and multichannel sales problems. Take steps to manage these risks.

7. Often considered unthinkable, dumping the wrong kinds of customers or partners is an essential part of becoming indispensable.

8. Know that a business will spoil any chance of becoming indispensable should it fall prey to any of the Seven Deadly Sins of indispensable change.

9. Never settle for "good enough!"

10. By keeping a steady foot on the accelerator and maintaining the "right" level of intensity, you will build the kind of customer relationships that last a lifetime. You will build the kind of business that we can call *indispensable*.

Epilogue
Just Keep It Real!

NOW THAT YOU'VE READ *INDISPENSABLE*, you probably have come to realize that leadership is simply about setting direction and managing change.

Forget what the leadership gurus have to say—many just complicate matters with jargon and fluff. Leadership boils down to defining a goal and navigating the path to achieve it. Therefore, if you want your business to become indispensable, you have to be ready to set that direction and manage all of the changes needed to get there. It is as simple as that!

In addition, by reading the book, you probably have come to realize I'm not one for hyperbole. Rather, I like to think that *I keep it real*. So it is in keeping with that spirit that I offer this final bit of advice: just be yourself.

In other words, strive to be an *authentic leader*.

So much of what we have discussed in these pages centers on trust. Without it, you're dead in the water. With it, there's hope that your team will pull together and do whatever it takes to make your business indispensable. But your staffers must trust you. If they don't, they won't give you their all. Indeed, they need to believe you, and believe in you, in order to perform at the level required for indispensability.

Here are a few ideas that may help you *keep it real* and become the kind of authentic leader needed to make your business indispensable.[1]

Be honest. Nothing kills a leader quicker than a reputation for being untrustworthy. Conversely, if you are unwaveringly honest all the time, you won't run that risk.

Consider Richard Branson for a moment. He is widely recognized as an inspiring leader who consistently "walks the talk" and takes full responsibility for his decisions—the good and the not-so-good. Anyone remember Virgin Digital? It was supposed to overtake iTunes. It didn't. But Branson took full responsibility for his company's foray into the space even when it proved to be a bust.

Talk straight. Keep your communications simple and to the point. Convoluted messaging just leads to confusion and misunderstanding. Talk straight and your people will know exactly what you mean.

Think of the frustration that most Americans feel when listening to our political leaders. The doublespeak, so common in political circles, is so bad that a recent poll conducted by Pew Research Center suggests that only 3 percent of Americans say that they can trust the government in Washington to do what is right "just about always."[2]

Don't be the kind of leader who prefers rhetoric to simply stating the facts.

Be you. Would you follow someone who is disingenuous? I wouldn't!

Steve Jobs was seen as brash and conceited. But his people adored working for him. They knew that they were always going to get Steve being Steve. It was reliable and true.

So be yourself. You being you should be enough to inspire others to follow your lead.

Be decisive. People want decisiveness in their leaders. Sure, take some time to gather insight and review the facts, then make the call. Your business will suffer if you delay.

In 1972, for example, Ford announced that all of its new cars would run on radials. Firestone, which sat atop the U.S. market at that time, didn't have a radial tire when Ford made their announcement. Seeing the rise in radial tires' popularity in Europe in the 1960s, Firestone was still contemplating whether they should make the necessary investment in this new kind of tire manufacturing. It was then that French company Michelin entered the U.S. market with their radial tires and began to dominate the world market as a result.

Don't let analysis paralysis keep you from making the call.

Be in it. The best leaders work right alongside the people they're leading.

Famously, Elon Musk has an undeniable work ethic, one that his people can only aspire to achieve. There are countless stories of him working so long and hard that he has to crawl into a corner somewhere in Tesla's facility to catch a nap.[3] He sets the example for his team.

Do not be above doing the work. Be right in it with your people and they will bust through brick walls for you.

Remember, *just keep it real* and you will do fine!

I wish you Godspeed in your journey to indispensability.

The Last Word

IF YOU LIKE THIS BOOK and are interested in instituting the Indispensable Agenda that is presented, I am available to provide consulting support and have developed a formal program that can help you do it.

The program will lead you and your organization through a planning process that covers the topics covered in the book. Together we will co-create an exciting plan specifically tailored to make your business indispensable.

For more information on this program or my availability for consultation, please contact me at jim@indispensable-consulting.com.

If you're interested in booking me to speak at your company or event in the U.S. please contact me directly. If you're interested in booking me for an event in Europe or Asia, please contact Joanna Jones of the Atlantic Speaker Bureau at jo@atlanticspeakerbureau.com, +44(0)1202 734 817.

Lastly, for additional information and content, please visit: https://indispensable-consulting.com/.

You can subscribe to the Indispensable Blog there too. It's free and a nice way to receive some extra value-added leadership ideas and insights.

Thank you!

Notes

Chapter 1

1 https://www.bloomberg.com/news/articles/2019-09-27/mylan-sued-by
-sec-over-failure-to-disclose-possible-loss.

2 https://www.washingtonpost.com/business/economy/2016/08/
25/7f83728a-6aee-11e6-ba32-5a4bf5aad4fa_story.html?postshare=
2121472232511539.

3 https://jobs.netflix.com/culture.

4 https://www.inc.com/alexa-von-tobel/alibaba-ceo-jack-ma-if-you-want
-your-life-to-be-simple-dont-be-the-leader.html.

5 https://www.inc.com/tommy-mello/microsoft-ceo-satya-nadella-just
-gave-best-leadership-advice-in-7-words.html.

6 https://twitter.com/cnbcevents/status/1113148994451116033.

7 https://people.com/human-interest/texas-roadhouse-ceo-kent-taylor
-gave-away-salary-bonus-of-800k-help-employees-pandemic/.

8 Derived from James M. Kerr, "So, You Want to Be a Disruptor?," Inc.com,
March 27, 2017.

9 https://www.bizjournals.com/dallas/news/2020/04/10/southwest
-airlines-employee-leave-coronavirus.html.

10 https://www.usatoday.com/story/money/business/2018/06/15/worst
-companies-to-work-for-employee-reviews/35812171/.

11 https://www.cnbc.com/2018/12/04/glassdoor-the-best-places-to-work
-in-2019.html.

12 https://lasvegassun.com/news/2020/jun/02/retail-therapy-zappos
-offers-to-listen-to-pandemic/.

13 https://www.forbes.com/sites/micahsolomon/2017/06/12/tony-hsieh
-spills-the-beans-the-one-word-secret-of-zappos-customer-service
-success/#340946b1accc.

14 https://www.amazon.com/Delivering-Happiness-Profits-Passion
-Purpose/dp/0446563048/.

15 https://www.pavingforpizza.com.

16 https://www.bigthinkedge.com/do-you-work-in-a-high-trust-or-low
    -trust-organization/.

17 https://www.bostonglobe.com/business/2019/02/08/feeling-emotional
    -the-machines-know/zWmGiTGC7jCtSI1TrnIs4O/story.html.

18 https://www.inc.com/minda-zetlin/jetblue-courtney-duffy-fired
    -bridesmaid-free-tickets.html.

19 https://www.fastcompany.com/90212570/elon-musk-drama-or-no-tesla
    -still-has-investors-on-its-side.

20 https://www.health.govt.nz/system/files/documents/publications/
    influenza-pandemic-plan-framework-action-2nd-edn-aug17.pdf.

21 Based on James M. Kerr, "5 Ways to Become Indispensable," Inc.com,
    July 6, 2016.

22 https://www.inc.com/john-koetsier/why-every-amazon-meeting-has-at
    -least-one-empty-chair.html.

23 https://smallbiztrends.com/2018/07/improving-the-customer
    -experience.html.

24 https://www.businessinsider.com/adidas-sneakers-plastic-bottles-ocean
    -waste-recycle-pollution-2019-8.

Chapter 2

1   James Charlton, *The Military Quotation Book* (New York: St. Martin's Press,
    1990), 83.

2   https://insiders.fortune.com/for-better-or-worse-a-consistent-leadership
    -style-is-key-to-success-25e71fcea78d.

3   https://www.youtube.com/watch?v=PznJqxon4zE.

4   https://hbr.org/2020/06/wolfgang-puck-on-leading-his-restaurants
    -through-the-pandemic.

5   https://www.virgin.com/branson-family/richard-branson-blog.

6   https://www.ttnews.com/articles/navistar-appoints-persio-lisboa
    -new-ceo.

7   https://www.benzinga.com/news/20/07/16632472/navistar-to-sell
    -driverless-semis-in-2024.

8   https://www.shrm.org/resourcesandtools/hr-topics/employee
    -relations/pages/these-companies-put-employees-first-during
    -pandemic.aspx.

9   https://www.wired.com/story/mark-zuckerberg-talks-to-wired-about
    -facebooks-privacy-problem/.

10 https://econtent.hogrefe.com/doi/abs/10.1027/2151-2604/a000189.

11 https://www.entrepreneur.com/slideshow/352216.

12 https://hbr.org/2010/05/need-speed-slow-down.

13 https://www.amazon.com/Its-Good-Be-King-Leadership/dp/
1541156463.

14 https://www.forbes.com/sites/lauragarnett/2020/04/16/how-these
-19-founders-and-ceos-are-leading-during-the-covid-19-crisis/
#1bddbaf84185.

15 https://www.fastcompany.com/90488060/our-offices-will-never-be-the
-same-after-covid-19-heres-what-they-could-look-like.

16 https://ravenind.com/news/raven-industries-receives-5-million-fema
-contract-award.

17 https://www.usatoday.com/story/money/business/2013/02/09/
founders-ruin-companies/1905921/.

Chapter 3

1 https://www.space.com/spacex-starlink-launch-fourth-rocket-landing
-success.html.

2 https://www.cbsnews.com/news/librarian-uses-drone-to-deliver-books
-to-kids-stuck-at-home-due-to-coronavirus/.

3 https://www.cnbc.com/2019/04/05/how-caspers-founders-built-a
-billion-dollar-mattress-start-up.html.

4 https://chiefexecutive.net/marriotts-arne-m-sorenson-2019-ceo-of
-the-year/.

5 Jeremy Hsu, "The Secrets of Storytelling: Why We Love a Good Yarn,"
Scientific American, August 2008, http://www.scientificamerican.com/
article/the-secrets-of-storytelling/.

6 https://www.forbes.com/sites/kpmg/2018/07/19/the-great-rewrite-the
-future-of-work-in-an-automated-world/#353045731105.

7 https://personality-insights-demo.ng.bluemix.net/.

Chapter 4

1 https://www.businessinsider.com/nadella-brilliant-jerk-phenom-in-tech
-is-done-2019-5.

2 https://247wallst.com/special-report/2018/06/07/worst-companies-to
-work-for/3/.

3 https://www.wsj.com/articles/ubers-hack-disclosure-raises-questions
-about-timing-1511462671.

4 https://www.inc.com/john-eades/chick-fil-a-opened-on-a-sunday-its-a
-brilliant-lesson-for-any-business.html?cid=search.

5 https://www.wsj.com/articles/gm-ceo-to-discuss-ignition-switch-probe
-findings-thursday-1401897900.

6   https://www.npr.org/2019/02/20/696198626/southwest-grounds
-planes-blames-labor-dispute-with-the-union.
7   https://ir.hubspot.com/news/hubspot-reports-q3-2019-results.
8   https://news.gallup.com/businessjournal/147383/secret-higher
-performance.aspx.
9   https://www.forbes.com/sites/deniselyohn/2018/09/12/advancing-a
-culture-of-education-at-ibm/#5b8e2f4c5265.
10   https://www.amazon.com/Hired-Months-Undercover-Low-Wage
-Britain/dp/1786490145.
11   https://technology.inquirer.net/55507/googles-culture-of
-innovation.
12   https://www.forbes.com/sites/micahsolomon/2018/09/30/how-to
-build-a-culture-of-customer-experience-innovation-the-usaa-way/
#9d360942378f.
13   https://www.usatoday.com/story/news/nation/2019/09/01/hurricane
-dorian-waffle-house-index-disasters/2187708001/.
14   https://www.cnbc.com/2020/04/15/hot-spots-of-innovation-as-a-result
-of-coronavirus-pandemic.html.

Chapter 5

1   https://news.gallup.com/poll/241649/employee-engagement-rise.aspx.
2   A. H. Maslow, "A Theory of Human Motivation," *Psychological Review* 50,
no. 4 (1943): 370–96.
3   https://www.cnbc.com/2019/10/07/comparably-top-100-companies
-with-best-compensation-2019.html.
4   https://www.octanner.com/case-studies/bdc.html.
5   https://www.entrepreneur.com/article/285052.
6   https://resources.kenblanchard.com/podcasts/how-to-help-your-leaders
-adapt-to-rapid-change-and-improve-engagement-with-jim-clifton.
7   https://medium.com/swlh/5-lessons-from-growing-the-skillshare-team
-to-50-8488adad9903.
8   http://emilydonato.blogspot.com/2013/06/nordstrom-culture.html.
9   http://www.enrich-hr.co.uk/blog/5-strategies-for-gee-great-employee
-engagement-by-sir-richard-branson.
10   James M. Kerr, "Hire Ambition: Because You Can't Teach Desire,"
Inc.com, July 13, 2015.
11   https://www.talentsmart.com/about/talentsmart.php.
12   https://electrek.co/2017/06/02/elon-musk-tesla-injury-factory/.
13   https://www.hsj.co.uk/leadership/charisma--humility--effective
-leadership-during-covid-19/7027795.article?adredir=1.

14 https://www.qualtrics.com/blog/customer-service-examples/.

15 https://blog.surveyjunkie.com/this-trader-joes-customer-service-story -will-make-your-day/.

16 https://www.forbes.com/sites/groupthink/2017/08/24/how-to-pay -employees-based-on-customer-feedback/#6853e51320b3.

17 https://hbr.org/2008/07/putting-the-service-profit-chain-to-work.

18 https://hbr.org/2019/06/every-new-employee-needs-an-onboarding -buddy.

19 https://studentloanhero.com/featured/companies-that-pay-off -student-loans/.

20 https://www.impactbnd.com/blog/how-to-get-your-team-to-create -content.

21 https://www.gartner.com/smarterwithgartner/diversity-and-inclusion -build-high-performance-teams/.

22 https://outleadership.com/.

23 https://emplify.com/blog/diversity-inclusion-culture-examples/.

24 https://www.potentialproject.com/leadership-development/developing -a-people-centered-culture-with-marriott/.

25 https://www.entrepreneur.com/article/249174.

26 https://www.gsb.stanford.edu/insights/what-it-be-owned-warren -buffett.

27 https://jobs.raytheon.com/work-life.

Chapter 6

1 https://www.huffpost.com/entry/worst-companies-to-work_for_n _575b26b0e4b0e39a28ada793.

2 https://www.prnewswire.com/news-releases/dish-network-reports-third -quarter-2019-financial-results-300953468.html.

3 https://www.usatoday.com/story/money/business/2018/06/15/worst -companies-to-work-for-employee-reviews/35812171/.

4 https://www.cnn.com/2019/12/11/business/ceo-departures-2019/ index.html.

5 https://hbr.org/2016/11/how-the-best-ceos-differ-from-average-ones.

6 https://www.cnn.com/2019/12/09/tech/away-luggage-ceo-steph-korey/ index.html.

7 https://www.nytimes.com/2019/10/22/business/nike-ceo-mark -parker.html.

8 https://hbr.org/2017/01/the-neuroscience-of-trust.

9 https://hbr.org/2019/12/to-build-a-strong-culture-create-rules-that-are -unique-to-your-company/.

10 Ibid.

11 Derived from James M. Kerr, "The 'Be Attitudes' of Building Trust in the Workplace," Inc.com, July 17, 2017.

12 https://www.researchgate.net/publication/228654971_Entrepreneurs _as_Authentic_Leaders_Impact_on_Employees'_Attitudes.

13 Bill George, *Discover Your True North*, expanded and updated edition (Hoboken, NJ: Wiley, 2015), 222.

14 https://iveybusinessjournal.com/publication/good-leaders-never-stop -learning/.

15 https://www.scoopwhoop.com/global-leaders-simple-living/.

16 https://www.sciencedirect.com/science/article/abs/pii/ S0191886915300659.

17 https://www.washingtonpost.com/news/business/wp/2018/05/ 02/african-american-men-arrested-at-starbucks-reach-1-settlement -with-the-city-secure-promise-for-200000-grant-program-for-young -entrepreneurs/.

18 https://www.inc.com/jim-schleckser/transparency-new-leadership -super-power.html.

19 https://www.inc.com/rana-el-kaliouby/how-to-be-an-empathetic-leader -in-times-of-crisis.html.

20 https://www.webershandwick.com/news/civility-in-america-2019 -solutions-for-tomorrow/.

Chapter 7

1 https://www.bloomberg.com/news/articles/2019-05-08/now-you-see-it -now-you-don-t-the-great-dismantling-of-siemens.

2 https://www.workforce.com/2016/02/05/ibm-sets-a-new-checkpoint/.

3 https://www.cdc.gov/coronavirus/2019-ncov/community/mental -health-non-healthcare.html.

4 Based on James M. Kerr, "Break Down the Silos for Sustainable Business Performance," Inc.com, May 18, 2015.

5 http://newsroom.pw.utc.com/news?item=123276.

6 https://www2.deloitte.com/us/en/insights/focus/human-capital -trends/2019/team-based-organization.html.

7 https://www.mckinsey.com/business-functions/organization/our -insights/to-emerge-stronger-from-the-covid-19-crisis-companies -should-start-reskilling-their-workforces-now#.

8 https://www.prnewswire.com/news-releases/johnson--johnson-human -performance-institute-launches-corporate-athlete-resilience-program -300444628.html.

9   https://www.forbes.com/sites/rodgerdeanduncan/2018/04/06/close
-encounters-leadership-and-handwritten-notes/#47cd8c1d3e96.

10 https://www.jpmorgan.com/news/how-jpmorgan-is-leading-the-digital
-revolution.

11 https://www.jpmorganchase.com/corporate/About-JPMC/ab-business
-principles.htm.

12 https://www2.deloitte.com/us/en/pages/about-deloitte/articles/
press-releases/deloitte-and-amazon-web-services-launch-smart
-manufacturing-cloud-applications.html.

13 https://blog.performyard.com/performance-management-at-tesla-what
-we-know.

Chapter 8

1   https://hbswk.hbs.edu/item/national-health-costs-could-decrease-if
-managers-reduce-work-stress.

2   https://www.thedetroitbureau.com/2019/03/bmw-reassigns-key
-management-responsibilities/.

3   https://www.vanityfair.com/news/2019/11/inside-the-fall-of-wework.

4   https://www.nytimes.com/2010/10/03/business/03digi.html.

5   Derived from James M. Kerr, "Top 10 Leadership Assessment Questions,"
Inc.com, August 8, 2016.

6   https://www.autonews.com/executives/factory-strategist-oliver-zipse
-offers-bmw-bold-way-forward.

7   https://www.forbes.com/sites/johnrex/2019/11/26/the-unexpected
-combination-for-mastering-executive-presence/#342ace709b46.

8   https://www.inc.com/gene-hammett/3-lessons-from-jack-welch-on
-leadership-that-you-dont-learn-in-business-school.html.

9   Ken Blanchard and Garry Ridge, *Helping People Win at Work: A Business
Philosophy Called "Don't Mark My Paper, Help Me Get an A"* (Upper Saddle
River, NJ: Pearson, 2009).

10 https://www.inc.com/marcel-schwantes/heres-a-top-10-list-of-the
-worlds-best-ceos-but-they-lead-in-a-totally-unique-wa.html.

11 https://hbr.org/2019/09/in-the-ecosystem-economy-whats-your
-strategy.

12 https://www.fieldglass.com/sites/default/files/2019-04/SAP-Fieldglass
-External-Workforce-Insights-2018-Executive-Summary.pdf.

13 https://www.cnbc.com/2019/02/22/bmw-daimler-team-up-on-ride
-sharing-other-mobility-services.html.

14 https://hbr.org/2008/04/the-right-way-to-manage-unprofitable
-customers.

15   Based on James M. Kerr, "When Companies Fire Their Customers,"
       Inc.com, June 12, 2017.

Epilogue

1   Derived from James M. Kerr, "5 Ways to Stop Talking and Start Leading
      Authentically," Inc.com, March 18, 2019, https://www.inc.com/james
      -kerr/5-ways-to-stop-talking-start-leading-authentically.html.
2   https://www.people-press.org/2019/04/11/public-trust-in-government
      -1958-2019/.
3   https://www.businessinsider.com/tesla-employee-stories-elon-musk
      -sleeping-at-work-2018-8.

Index

abstract thinking, 28
accountability, 17, 31, 141, 183
achievability, 30
active listening, 43
Adidas, 21
Adobe, 126
Aetna, 120
Affectiva, 149
agility, 6
Alibaba Group, 4
alignment, 157, 171, 173
Allstate, 191
Alphabet, 56
Amazon, xiv, 29, 51, 84, 159
ambition, 111–12, 128, 166
analysis paralysis, 42
anticipation, 19, 21, 30, 47
anxiety, 132, 151
Apple, 2, 26–27, 108, 144, 180, 189
Apple Store, 21
Ardern, Jacinda, 47, 114
AT&T, 190
authenticity, 140–41, 199
authority, 37
Away, 133
AXA Equitable Insurance Company,
    147

Ballmer, Steve, 182
Belichick, Bill, 5, 93
belonging, 106, 165
benefits, 105
Benioff, Marc, xiv, 26
Berkshire Hathaway, 126
best and brightest, 80, 125
Bezos, Jeff, xiv, 21, 29
Blake, Frank, 182
Blakely, Sara, 31
blame, 16, 148
BMW, 179, 181–82, 189–90
Boeing, 2
bottlenecks, 159, 160–61
boundarylessness, 162, 174
Branson, Richard, 22, 29, 110, 200
breakthrough thinking, 42
Brin, Sergey, 34
Brindamour, Charles, 143
Brown, Chris, 186
buddies, 119
Buffett, Warren, 126
burnout, 83–84, 100, 127, 178–79
business life, 120, 125
business-to-business (B2B)
    relationships, 187–90, 197
buy-in, 59, 66, 68, 75, 76

Campbell Soup, 169
Capital One, 105
career paths, 105–6
Casper, 57
CA Technologies, 117
change adaptability, 95–96
change fatigue, 97, 101
change management, 23, 74, 153, 170–74
character, 25–26
charisma, 115
Chesapeake Energy, 51
Clarke, Troy, 30
Clifton, Jim, 107–8
coaching, xv, 46–47, 145, 148, 168, 183, 185
Coca-Cola Company, 127
cocreation, 99, 101, 115
Cogito, 14
collaboration, xv, 81, 115
comfort zone, 19, 156
commitment, xiv, 29, 36, 101, 118, 196
  lack of, 79–80
common decency, 9
communication, xiv, 49–50, 77–78, 113, 155, 182
  conventions for, 171–72
  effectiveness of, 182–83
  engagement and, 47
  lack of, 81, 194
  transparent, 17, 34, 138–40, 152
company affiliation, 79–80, 100
compensation, 105
competitiveness, 6, 9
Conant, Doug, 169
Conaway, Charles, 32
confidence, 29, 34, 124, 182
  of customers, 15
  of employees, 17, 33
conflict resolution, 113
Connecticut Department of Revenue Services, 65–66

connection, 35, 81, 144
consistency, 17, 26
continuous planning and execution, 18–20
conviction, 26, 52
cop-outs, 32–35
coronavirus pandemic, 38, 41, 56, 158
  employees during, 5, 8, 33
  impact of, 70–71, 97–98, 163, 166
  leadership during, 149, 182–83
  preparedness for, 18, 47
  responses to, xiv, 11, 46, 49, 96, 115
  work safety and, 47–48, 64–65, 79
Costco, 110
courage, 27, 52
COVID-19. *See* coronavirus pandemic
Crocker, Dave, 186
cult of personality, 59, 75
cultural levers, 92–97, 101
culture, 3, 4, 6, 22, 79–84
  cultivation of, 100
  diversity and, 122
  importance of, 77–78
  influences on, 100
  toxic, 81, 133
Culture Baseline, 87–88
Culture Gap Analysis, 89–90
Culture Reset™ Methodology, 84–93
Culture Reset™ Plan, 90, 101
Culture Reset™ Principles, 86–87
Culture Reset™ Story, 88–89
Culture Transformation Plan, 84–85
Cuomo, Andrew, 182–83
customer experience, 6, 9, 13, 58
"customer first" attitude, 10, 32, 116–18, 128, 146
customer intimacy, 21, 22, 23, 78
customers
  choices of, 15, 22
  communication with, 19
  emphasis on, 30
  expectations of, 14, 22
  feedback from, 21
  focus on, 15

customers *(continued)*
  interactions with, 6, 9–10
  internal, 117
  potential of, 3–4
  prioritizing, 20, 21
  treatment of, 2, 7, 8, 9
  wants of, 3–5
customer satisfaction, 116, 147
customer service, 11, 12, 14–15, 92,
  116–18, 173

Daimler, 189–90
decision-making, 4, 6, 23, 27,
  36–37, 52
  approaches to, 42
  clarity in, 135
  diversity and, 121
  employee-driven, 146
  empowerment and, 110
  fearlessness in, 40–42
  participation in, 109
decision rights, 37, 147, 186
decisiveness, 200
Deep, Danny, 19, 93
delegation, 39, 135
*Delivering Happiness: A Path to
  Profits, Passion, and Purpose*
  (Hsieh), 12
Deloitte, 161–62
Delta Air Lines, 8
dependability, 137, 187
dialogue, 19, 60, 149
  open and honest, 113, 150, 152
differentiation, 3, 12, 22, 94
digital capabilities, 69–70, 76, 96,
  101, 164
diligence, 135, 193–94
Dimon, Jamie, 19, 171
direction-setting, xiv, xv, 28, 31,
  199
discipline, 193–94
discontent, expression of, 150, 152
Discover Your True North (George),
  141–42

DISH Network Corporation, 132
Disney, 29, 57
disruption, 3, 4, 7, 144
dissent, encouragement of, 42–45, 52
diversity, 79, 121–23, 129
Domino's, 13

Easterbrook, Fred, 17
ecosystems, 187–90, 197
EDA Inc., 46
el Kaliouby, Rana, 149
emotional intelligence quotient (EQ),
  33, 112–16, 128
empathy, 13, 58, 114, 149, 182
employee development, 4–5
employee engagement, 33, 98, 101
employees, 11–12, 19, 29, 34–35
  empowerment of, 4
  focus and, 165–66
  frontline, 13, 14, 60, 139
  support for, 5
  treatment of, 7–8
employee satisfaction, 117
  lack of, 80
employee value proposition (EVP),
  104–7, 128
employers of choice, 78
empowerment, 4, 23, 36, 126, 131
  importance of, 148
  institutionalizing, 145–48
  lack of, 82, 135
enablement, 82, 126
encouragement, 182
engagement, 47, 66, 154–55
  lack of, 135
Enterprise, 80
enthusiasm, 27, 52
EQ. *See* emotional intelligence
  quotient
esprit de corps, 93, 150
Estée Lauder, 120
esteem, 106
ethics, 195
EVP. *See* employee value proposition

excellence, 3, 93, 138, 149, 151, 196
    focus on, 163–64
execution, 18, 49, 67
    destabilized, 99
expectations, 146, 186–87

Fabletics, 70
fabrication, 16–17
Facebook, 17, 30, 33–34, 41–42
fair-mindedness, 9
fairness, 8, 26, 126
Fauci, Anthony, 141
fear, 41, 42
fearlessness, 40–42
feedback, 21, 35, 83, 158, 183
fit, 181–84
"flavor of the month" mentality,
    98–99, 101
flipping the pyramid. *See* pyramid:
    inverted
focus, 157, 165–66, 186
focusing on the outside, 108, 128
focus orientation, 93, 101
followership, 25, 33, 52, 115, 169,
    182
Ford, 200–201
Franz, Steve, 194
free will, 145–46

Gallup, 83, 104, 107–8
Gartner, 121
Geico, 22
General Dynamics Land Systems
    (GDLS), 37, 68, 138–39, 140, 151,
    154–55, 172, 186
    leadership at, 19, 93, 170, 187
    vision story of, 62–63, 67, 73–74,
        193
General Electric (GE), 157
General Motors, 81
George, Bill, *Discover Your True North*,
    141–42
Gilbert, Dan, 138
give and take, 108–9

Glazer, Jeffrey, 59, 60
global marketplace, 121–22
goals, xiv–xv, 23, 29, 126
    definition of, 144
    financial, 63
    short-term, 158
going above and beyond, 22, 110
Goldenberg, Adam, 70
Golden Rule of Indispensability, 7–8,
    9, 23
Google, 34–35, 56, 94
governance, 91, 159
grace under pressure, 114
graciousness, 9
greater good, 50–51, 53
greed, 180–81

Hagemann, Bonnie, 46
hand-offs, 159, 161
Harder, Ron, 169–70
Hartford, The, 67, 146–47, 184–85,
    186, 193
Harvard Business Review, 40, 133, 135
Hastings, Reed, 4, 31
Hees, Bernardo, 132
Helping People Win at Work (Ridge and
    Blanchard), 183
hero disease, 178–79
Hertz, 80
Holmes, Elizabeth, 16
Home Depot, The, 165, 182
honesty, 26, 52, 200
Hsieh, Tony, 12
Hubspot, 82
Huffington Post, 132
humility, 142

IBM, 4–5, 83, 157–58
identification, 75
Iger, Bob, 29, 57
imagination, 56
Impact, 120
inclusion, 121–23
indecisiveness, 41–42

indispensability
  as choice, 15–18
  definition of, 1, 22
  elements of, 20
  fundamentals of, 21
  Golden Rule of, 7–8, 9, 23
  leadership and, 25
  outside perspective on, 13
  vision and, 75
Indispensable Agenda, 20
"in it together" philosophy, 13
innovation, 7, 42, 56, 57, 78, 94
innovation leverage, 94–95
inspiration, 16, 25, 27, 28, 29, 33, 34
Intact Financial Corporation, 143
integrity, 15, 17, 18, 23, 33, 140–43,
    182
  building of, 152
  See also trustworthiness
investment, 30, 49
Ishmael, Don, 19

JetBlue, 13
jettisoning, 190–92, 197
Jewelers Mutual, 65, 169–70, 193–94
Jobs, Steve, 26–27, 28, 108, 144, 180,
    200
job satisfaction, 34, 103–4
Johnson, Jim, 123, 147–48
Johnson, Kevin, 115, 148
Johnson & Johnson, 167–68
JPMorgan Chase (JPM), 19, 171, 172
JustFab Inc., 69–70

Kaeser, Joe, 156–57, 160
Kalanick, Travis, 80
Karnjanaprakorn, Michael, 108–9,
    194
keeping it real, 45, 141, 199
keeping it simple, 45–48
Kelly, Gary, 8
Kennedy, John F., 39–40
Khosrowshahi, Dara, 80
Kmart, 32

Korey, Steph, 133
Kotchman, Don, 187
Kraft Heinz Company, 132–33
Krim, Philip, 57
Krüger, Harald, 179

Laguarta, Ramon, 33
leadership
  absentee, 34
  attributes of, 5–6
  behavior and, 171
  as choice, 46, 48, 51, 53
  compelling, 169–70, 175
  development of, 184–87
  empowered, 147–48
  by example, xiii, 115, 196
  interactive, 36
  vs. management, 28–32, 52
  personal styles, 45
  teams, 181–84
  tendencies, 92–93
learning, 46, 142–43, 165–66
learning organizations, 41, 45
Lenovo, 122
less is more, 38–39
leverage, 10, 157, 163
Lewis, Kristy, 38
LexisNexis, 59, 60–61, 62, 69, 139–40,
    166, 193, 195
Lisboa, Persio, 30
listening, 142, 182
Lokerse, Jeroen, 47–48
loyalty, 8

Ma, Jack, 4
Mackey, John, 51
management, 27, 28–32, 52
Marinello, Kathryn, 80
Marriott, Bill, 125–26
Marriott International, 58, 125–26
Marsh & McLennan, 191
Maslow's hierarchy of needs, 104–5
McClendon, Aubrey, 51
Mendoza, Tom, 35

mentorship, 6, 119, 123–25, 129,
    147–48
MetLife, 14
metrics, 11, 15
Michelin, 201
micromanagement, 34, 126, 180
Microsoft, 4, 79, 119, 182
middle management, 59–60, 66–67,
    68–69, 75–76
mistakes, learning from, 23, 41, 150
Mitsui Sumitomo Insurance Group,
    36, 66, 69, 139, 150, 165, 170
modesty, 124, 128
Moonves, Les, 17
morale, 99, 132, 149, 151, 191
motivation, 25, 33, 146, 175
Mujica, José, 143
Mulcahy, Anne, 141–42
Murakami, Haruki, 170
Musk, Elon, 16, 28, 113–14, 171, 201
Musk, inside, 56
mutual benefits, 188
Mylan, 2

Nadella, Satya, 4, 79
narcissism, 35
narrative, changing of, 100, 101
National Health System (England),
    115
Nationwide, 191
Navistar International, 30
NBA, 41
Nespresso, 187–88
NetApp, 35
Netflix, 4, 29, 31
Netherlands Cushman &
    Wakefield, 47
Neumann, Adam, 180
New England Patriots, 5, 93
New Zealand, 18, 47, 114
NeXT Computer, 180
Next-Gen workforce, 118–20, 129
    leader development, 184–87, 197
Nicholson, Pam, 80

Nike, 134
Nordstrom, 109, 116
Nvidia, 120

opaqueness, 17
open-door policy, 34, 151, 186
operating principles, 42, 135
opportunity, 41–42
    lack of, 83
organizational design, 157, 159, 161,
    172–73
organizations, 31
outcomes, 186
Out Leadership, 122
outside perspective, 13, 18–19
overmanagement, 178–81, 196
ownership, 154

Page, Larry, 34
Parker, Mark, 134
participation, 154–55
passion, 26–27
patience, 179
PepsiCo, 33, 149
perfection, 20
performance, 49, 150
    evaluation of, 157–58
    measurement of, 14, 146
    rewards for, 117
personal action reminders, 136
personality, 32, 52
    of organizations, 72–74, 76
personality theory, 73–74, 76
Peterson, Joel, 13
Pettersen, Helen, 115
Pferdt, Frederik, 94
Pichai, Sundar, 35
Plan Governance Framework, 91, 101
pocket vetoes, 37
potholes, 97–100, 101
Pratt & Whitney, 161
preparation, 35–36, 52
price, 12, 23
principles, 26, 85, 86–87

proactivity, 34
product, 12, 23
productivity, 132, 151
progress, 11
Project Brief Template, 89–90
promise keeping, 22
promise-keeping, 137–38, 151, 172, 189
providers of choice, 3–4
Puck, Wolfgang, 27
Purdue Pharma, 180–81
push, 97–98
pyramid, 66–68, 131
    inverted, 109, 116, 128

Quicken Loans, 137–38
Quinn Snacks, 38

"rank and yank" system, 157, 173
Raven Industries, 48–49
Raytheon, 127
reaction time, 41
readiness, 173
recognition, 83, 105–6, 117, 127, 145, 150, 169
reliability, 26, 30, 141
reliance, 22
reputation, 106, 191
resiliency, 37, 78, 158, 166–69, 175
respect, 9, 26, 142, 152
responsibility, 6, 16, 23, 26, 31, 37, 141
    bifurcation and, 159, 174
    clarification of, 165
responsiveness, 41
Ressler, Don, 70
restructuring, 179
retention, 80
rewards, 35, 127, 145, 157, 183
Ridge, Garry, 183
right-sizing, 157
risk appetite, 93–94, 101
risk-taking, 31
roll-out schedules, 69

Rometty, Virginia, 4–5
Ruffolo, Bob, 120
Rykhus, Daniel A., 48–49

Salesforce, xiv, 26
Sandberg, Sheryl, 17
scalability, 188–89
Schwartz, Mark, 32
Schwartzott, Paul, 185, 186
Schwarzkopf, Norman, 25
Screwfix, 106
self-actualization, 106–7
self-awareness, 124
self-centeredness, 15–16
self-confidence, 181
self-importance, 133
self-interest, 51, 53
selfishness, 50, 53, 181
self-management, 173
self-promotion, 133
self-sufficiency, 143–45, 148
Semel, Terry, 41–42
service businesses, 9–10
service delivery, 12–15, 23, 116–18, 192
setbacks, 46
Seven Deadly Sins of indispensable change, 192–95, 197
Siemens AG, 156–57, 160
silos, 81, 159–63, 174
Silver, Adam, 41
Skillshare, 108–9, 194
Smart Health Clubs, 96
social impact, 96–97
socialization, 51
solo artistry, 179–80
Sorenson, Arne, 58
Southwest Airlines, 7, 82, 118
SpaceX, 28, 56
Spanx, 31
sponsorship, 154, 174, 194
Sprint, 190
staff. *See* employees
Starbucks, 114–15, 148

Stein, Gordon, 151
stickiness, 22, 120, 158–59, 174
storytelling, 74, 88, 169–70
straight talk, 200
strategic alignment, 77, 92, 158
   lack of, 81
strategic execution, 68
strategic guideposts, 130–40
strategic planning, 18–20
strategic platform, 74, 76
strategic thrust, 138–39
stress, 34, 39, 167, 179
structured methodology, 99
student loan relief, 120
Stumpf, John, 16
Sullivan, Kevin, 65–66
synergy, 57

tact, 114
talent, 4–5, 6, 157, 183, 184–85,
   194–95
talent magnets, 78, 125–27
TalentSmart, 113
targets, 29, 192
Taylor, Kent, 5
teaching, 11, 36, 45, 68, 142–43, 183
team-based structures, 161–62
teams, 23, 148, 180
   development of, 6
   dissent and, 42–44
   of leaders, 35–38, 181–84, 196
   support for, xv
teamwork, xv, 77, 189–90
   lack of, 81
technology, 2, 30, 146–47, 164, 172
   integrative, 189
tenacity, 29, 49, 124–25
Tesla Motors, 56, 113–14, 171, 173
Texas Roadhouse, 5
Theranos, 16
Toyota, 81
Trader Joe's, 117
training, 64–65, 71, 83, 86, 120,
   165–66, 167–69

transformation, xiv, 5, 6, 7, 154
transformation programs, 154, 160,
   161
transparency, 36, 39, 138–40,
   149
   in B2B relationships, 189–90
   in communication, 17, 34, 152
   lack of, 135
trust, 15, 18, 36, 77, 131, 196
   in B2B relationships, 189–90
   building of, 45, 134–37, 142, 152,
      182
   of customers, 23
   among employees, 12, 13, 14, 36
   importance of, 148
   lack of, 80, 134
   in leaders, 17, 26, 34, 199
   loss of, 47
   measurement of, 136
   training and, 136
trust breakdowns, 134–35
trust prompts, 136
trust quotient, 136
trust values, 135
trustworthiness, 135, 137. *See also*
   integrity
Tsujihara, Kevin, 17

Uber, 80–81, 195
uncertainty, 29, 37, 141, 150
underdog mentality, 108
underperformance, 79, 157
understanding, xv, 12, 30–31
   lack of, 81
United Airlines, 3
unpredictability, 17
USAA, 94–95
U.S. Marine Corps (USMC), 106–7

values, 8–9, 61, 106, 116–18, 167, 172.
   See also trust values
Vertafore, 144
Virgin, 29, 110
Virgin Hotels, 22

vision, xiv–xv, 6, 23, 29–30
  achievement of, 5, 7
  development of, 51, 55–58
  presentation of, 47
  recommitment to, 156
  shaping of, 59–61
vision statements, 62
vision stories, 60, 61–63, 71–73,
    74–76, 107–8, 125, 130–40
  audiences for, 66–67, 75
  coronavirus pandemic and, 70–71
  creation of, 59, 62–65, 75
  development of, 75
  dimensions of, 64
  formats of, 76, 193
  importance of, 192–93
  socializing of, 65–66
Volkswagen, 3
von Rueden, Anton, 70

Wade, Heather, 37
Waffle House, Inc., 95–96
WAIT acronym (Why Am I Talking),
    145
Wall Street Journal, 80
Warsteiner Group, 96–97

WD-40 Company, 183
Weber Shandwick, 149
Welch, Jack, 157
Wells Fargo, 3, 16–17
WeWork, 180
Whited, Gary, 37, 67, 68, 93, 170
Whole Foods, 51
"why not?" questions, 55–56
Wing, 56
working remotely, 71, 82, 163
work/life balance, 83–84, 127
work setting, 10, 106, 121, 127, 148,
    152, 162–64
workshops, 59–60, 88, 155

Xerox, 141–42

Yahoo, 41–42
Yoshida, Koji, 36, 150, 170

Zappos, 10, 11, 12, 92, 110, 146,
    172–73, 194
Zipse, Oliver, 179, 181–82
Zoom Video Communications, xiii,
    144
Zuckerberg, Mark, 17, 30, 33–34, 42

More Titles From Humanix Books You May Be Interested In:

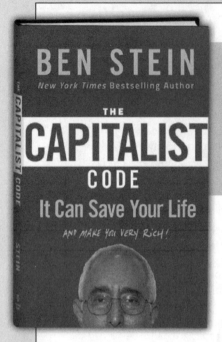

Warren Buffett says:

"My friend, Ben Stein, has written a short book that tells you everything you need to know about investing (and in words you can understand). Follow Ben's advice and you will do far better than almost all investors (and I include pension funds, universities and the super-rich) who pay high fees to advisors."

In his entertaining and informative style that has captivated generations, beloved *New York Times* bestselling author, actor, and financial expert Ben Stein sets the record straight about capitalism in the United States — it is not the "rigged system" young people are led to believe.

Scott Carpenter, Astronaut, NASA's Mercury Project says:

"By following the advice in The Simple Heart Cure, you can surmount the biggest challenge of all and win your battle against heart disease."

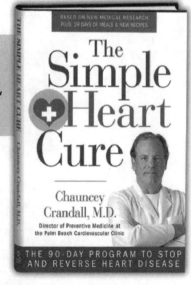

Heart disease kills more people than any other medical condition. In *The Simple Heart Cure*, you'll find this top doc's groundbreaking approach to preventing and reversing heart disease — an approach honed by his study of foreign cultures free of heart disease and decades of experience helping patients achieve a healthier heart at any age.